THE COURAGEOUS *life*

Learn Before You Leap

COURAGE

Melissa J. Nixon

AUTHOR ACADEMY elite

Rich,

You are one connected to amazing people like Kimberly. I know that Cal will do amazing things in your life. I wish you the best in your new endeavor. People are watching you. Keep courage,

Melissa

THE COURAGEOUS LIFE:

HOW TO LEAP FROM YOUR CAREER TO YOUR CALLING

Melissa J. Nixon

Scripture quotations are from The Holy Bible, New International Version® Copyright ©1973, 1978, 1984 by the International Bible Society.

Printed in the United States of America
2016 First Edition

Subject Index:
Nixon, Melissa J.
Title: The Courageous Life: How to Leap From Your Career to Your Calling
1. Career 2. Christian 3. Inspirational 4. Purpose 5. Self-Help

Paperback ISBN: 1943526303
EPub ISBN: 9781943526307
Hardback ISBN: 978-1-943526-31-4
Library of Congress Control Number: 2016905588
Author Academy Elite, Powell, OH

Author Academy Elite

COURAGEOUS PRAISES...

"This book is a needed resource and coaching tool for those looking to make a significant difference with their lives. Melissa shows up courageously and inspires all of us to do the same in our own lives."

Jennifer Keitt, Nationally Syndicated Radio Host, Author & Coach

"Melissa is the ultimate example of what happens when grace meets guts! She is a master at helping people trust God while they also navigate the ups and downs of change and transition. Her book elegantly guides readers into a place of purpose, surrender and authenticity. What I love about this book is that it is designed to help everyday women live the life God intends...not just in the future, but right now! This book is a life changer!"

Marshawn Evans Daniels, The Godfidence Coach
TV Personality from The Apprentice & Miss America Finalist

"Melissa J. Nixon is one who can attach herself to your divine purpose and see it through to fruition. We have witnessed her vision soar into her purpose. She has taken the leap from corporate to her life's destiny, which is no easy feat. But we can assure you that when the time is right and you take the first step, what is waiting for you will be beyond your wildest imagination. The process is difficult and the road can sometimes be rough, and even when we're faced with those times, we still hear Melissa's voice telling us to, "Own our seat at the table," "You belong there," "Live courageously," and "Believe God for what seems impossible!" Can you hear God calling you? Do you trust Him? Melissa's words of encouragement in this book are so profound. When you read it, your life will never be the same and you will be armed with everything you need to leap from your career to your calling."

Kelli Fisher and Tana Gilmore, The Matchmaking DUO
Author, **Relationship DUOvers**

"If you've ever found yourself shrinking away from all it is you were created to be, this book provides the roadmap to your destiny."

Avis A. Jones-DeWeever, Ph.D.
Author, **How Exceptional Black Women Lead**

The Courageous Life: How to Leap From Your Career to Your Calling unpacks our aspiring dreams and empowers us to move into our purpose no matter how lofty or how crazy it sounds. Each page that is read compels you to move from your comfort zone to a courageous life. Get ready to discover, declare, develop and determine that you will leap from your career to your calling! This book is going to transform lives!!

Adrienne S. Young,
Certified John Maxwell Speaker, Trainer, & Coach

This book is dedicated to

all the dreamers who have the courage to leap!

And to my dad,

I know you are smiling in heaven.

I love you...

MIRROR, MIRROR...

Are You:
The Dreamer
The Creative
The Student
The Entrepreneur
The Career-Minded
The Stay-at-Home Mom
The Retiree
The Person in Transition
The Believer?

If you identify with any one, or a combination of these characteristics, then this book is for you! Most of all, it's for anyone who dares to believe that God can change his or her life to make a bigger impact in the world.

TABLE OF CONTENTS

FOREWARD

Maybe you've heard the phrase "look before you leap?" It's usually positioned as an old proverb cautioning us to weigh the risks before we make a major change. Last time I checked, this advice provides little more than a hollow warning for those interested in going from their career to calling. Today's professionals need a proven way forward. We need to *learn* before we leap, especially if we hope to land safely.

The Courageous Life does just this. Author Melissa J. Nixon writes from a place of empathy and insight. She knows the path because she's walked the path. *The Courageous Life* provides a fresh framework for exactly how to make the leap from your day job to dream job. Each page fortifies your faith and reveals how to make an intelligent transition. Written in a candid style, Melissa offers sound advice free of pretense and platitudes.

The Courageous Life shares the steps you need to catapult you from sitting on the sidelines of your dreams to living with a sense of urgency and commitment.

Besides wisdom forged from her own leap, Melissa also includes real-life stories from close to a dozen ladies just like you. Isn't it time you left your corporate comfort zone, embraced your purpose, and launched into your destiny, once and for all? Discover how to transcend your insecurities, overcome your fears, and plow through your courage blocker™. *The Courageous Life* helps you leap from your career to your calling.

Read it and your life may change. Apply it and you'll change the lives of many others.

Kary Oberbrunner

CEO of Redeem the Day and Igniting Souls.
Co-creator of Author Academy Elite.
Author of *Day Job to Dream Job, The Deeper Path*, and *Your Secret Name*

Introduction

My 12th Grade Dream

*"Most people say they don't know what they want
to do in spite of their career, because they failed to
yield to the possibilities of the wonderful ideas that
run across their hearts and minds each day."*

Have you ever found yourself stuck in the middle of a career crisis? Asking yourself, "What do I want to be when I grow up?" Does it seem like you are dangling somewhere between a successful career that you've built and a passion that seems to be tugging at your heart? It is a complex question that it is often hard to boil down to one-word answers such as a writer, an engineer, a teacher, a social worker, or an entrepreneur. The lack of a meaningful transition strategy oftentimes results in responses such as, "I don't know what I want to do next" or "I don't know how to make *that* happen."

If you are like me, the answer has changed a number of times over the course of your life. I went from wanting to be a lawyer when I was eight, to an accountant when I was in high school, and then an industrial organizational psychologist, when I went to college. Suffice it to say, a few other career possibilities have been thrown into the mix of all of those. I finally landed in a fulfilling and successful human resources career which became a journey that I loved. Yet, even after a few years, that wasn't it. I found myself with this tug in my heart to do something even more purposeful, more impactful. Can you relate?

Over time, I realized that there are two groups of people: those that know what they want to do and those that don't. However, I personally believe that the group who says they do not know, actually really knows. It's just that the elements of fear, uncertainty, and family responsibilities, either stall or completely stop their pursuit of it. To say you "don't know" means you've never had one encounter with an idea or experience that sparked your interest. Even in the midst of writing this book, I've had several conversations with people who emphatically stated they do not know what they want to do next. However, when I pressed them about it, most told me that there has always been this "thing" (sometimes a couple of "things") that they've thought about doing, but never really followed through on them over the years. Common hindrances expressed were:

- They didn't know how
- It seemed unrealistic
- It was an untraditional path that would be difficult to follow

As you see, it's not because they never had an idea or inkling. Instead, it's because they had yet to yield to the possibility of the ideas that ran across their heart and mind. More importantly, they had yet to yield to the process of what it would take to get from where they were to where they wanted to be. I experienced similar feelings of uncertainty and intimidation with my own idea many years ago. No matter what career field I landed in, I knew that I eventually wanted to start my own personal development company to inspire, teach, and train others. I wanted to travel the world speaking and teaching on stages large and small, inspiring others to be their best selves.

This was the vision that occurred to me sitting in my bedroom during my senior year of high school. I literally saw myself standing on stage in front of thousands of people sharing exactly what each person needed to hear. An impactful message of hope, inspiration, and encouragement; the key elements to move forward. It became what I call *My 12th Grade Dream*. I never shared it with anyone at the time, but the seed was planted.

Like most, it seemed too lofty of an idea at such a young age, so I did what most people do. I followed a traditional career path. I went to college, went to graduate school, enrolled in more school, climbed the corporate ladder, and chased one promotion after the next. Through it all, God always had a funny way of letting me know that my time was up in every role and company. My prayer was always, "Never let me stay longer than I am supposed to, and never let me leave before it's my time." I knew that each place or position was purposeful, but it was only a part of my story.

With each new promotion and salary increase, I realized I was stuck in the pain of my own comfort. My comfortable career and salary made it easy for a cozy lifestyle filled with great dinners, the best shopping trips, and amazing vacations. Still, there was *My 12th Grade Dream,* etched in my heart. A picturesque sight which I had no clue how to bring to life. It was a place that I knew I needed to be, but a journey that I was not sure I was willing to take. It is often our lack of discomfort that causes us to miss the very thing we are supposed to do. I had a six-figure salary, generous bonuses, and corporate plane access. It was enough to make anyone think twice about stepping into the abyss of the unknown. It wasn't until I realized there was no salary or job title that could take away the growing discontentment in my heart that caused me to pursue my dream. I knew I had to either take a leap of faith and do something different, or stay unfulfilled.

Like me, something keeps telling you that where you are is not it. You have this looming, nagging, uncomfortable feeling that this is not where you are supposed to be, especially not forever. Or, you might be a work in progress, but you know that you could be doing more. For many, these feelings are not new. It's just that the level of comfort that we have established for ourselves is far too great to let go, and more than likely too rewarding to allow even the most conservative interruption.

> *"Every move of elevation will always require some level of discomfort as you leave what it is familiar to what it is unknown."*

For some, there comes a season where what we desire becomes less of a distant dream and more of a mandate. It can even feel like a responsibility that makes all of your current levels of comfort, certainty, and security worth the risk. You realize that it is not about keeping the comfortable life you have built intact. Instead, it is about completely disrupting it in order to live the courageous and meaningful life you were meant to live. You now see that you must make sacrifices that come with transition. More than likely, you have that same ache and discontentment in your heart that I had since *My 12th Grade Dream.* As I mentioned, many of you know exactly what God is calling you to. Others know that there is something more, but are not sure exactly what that "something" might be.

Either way, this book is for you, because the process to leap from your career to your calling is the same. No matter the circumstances, making the transition involves four key phases:

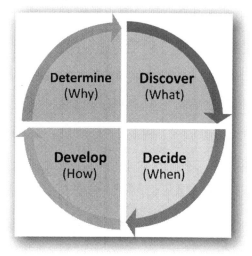

1. **Discovering** Where You're Going
2. **Deciding** Your Declaration to say, "Yes!"
3. **Developing** a Plan to Get There
4. **Determining** Your Staying Power

"Do not remember the former things,
nor consider the things of old.
*Behold, I will do a **new thing**, now it shall spring forth;*
Shall you not know it?
I will even make a road in the wilderness
and rivers in the desert."
- ISAIAH 43:18-19

This was the passage that God gave me to include in our senior vault during my last year of high school. It's amazing how *My 12th Grade Dream* continues to impact my life. Thank you God, for always helping me to remember that I was to never settle, but to diligently pursue the things you had for me. This book is not filled with perfect stories or precise formulas for overnight success. Instead, it is filled with relevant experiences and lessons that each of you can relate to and immediately apply as you start or continue your own courageous journey. You will see that some of the chapters contain a "Walking Out" section with a few key thoughts to carry you to the next step. I look forward to sharing strategies, tools, and thought-provoking questions that you need to consider as you leap from your career to your calling.

Welcome to this purposeful, bold walk, as you take these courageous steps to live *The Courageous Life*. If you dare to trust God to do a new thing in your life, career, or business, then keep reading!

PRAYER FOR THE JOURNEY

"Spirit lead where my trust is without borders
Let me walk upon the waters
Wherever You would call me
Take me deeper than my feet could ever wander
"Oceans" – Hillsong United

PART I

DISCOVER YOUR PURPOSE
(THE WHAT)

THE COURAGEOUS LIFE:

How to Leap from Your Career to Your Calling

> **Definition:**
> ***Courage*** - The ability to do
> something that you know is difficult
> or dangerous

When I take a look at my own personal journey of moving from my career to my calling, these four stages were critical in getting me to the point of having a story to tell. The journey is not as smooth as the diagram looks, nor will yours be. Mine took nearly 20 years from the time the seed was planted, to the time that I finally discovered the courage to do it. I wish I could tell you how long each phase takes, or when you will reach your goal, but that's totally up to you. More importantly, it is up to the level of trust you are willing to build with God, along with the faith and courage required to act it out. Congratulations, you have already taken the first *courageous* step!

COURAGEOUS STEP #1

WHAT'S NEXT, GOD?

Discovering Your Purpose

*"Being overwhelmed with the big picture
... can hinder you from being in the picture at all."*

In the past few years, it never fails that there is one curious person in my audience that is brave enough to ask me, "How did you know that this is what you wanted to do?" Even on a road trip with a girlfriend who has a great career, and thrives because she is doing what she knows, once turned to me and asked, "But, *Melissa, how did you know?*"

I would love to say, "I just knew." But that's not true. Sometimes, it does feel that way, since it's been such a long journey – dating back to that fateful day of *My 12th Grade Dream.* Truthfully, the answer is simple. I listened. I listened to my heart and didn't treat those wild and crazy "what if" daydreams as fleeting thoughts. Even more importantly, I followed the clues. I knew those thoughts and daydreams would take me somewhere if I earnestly followed the path. I never let go of that image of me standing before large audiences speaking, training, and encouraging people to their next level of success. Instead of me letting it go, I pursued it.

However, I've heard the question and had the conversation enough times to understand the question behind the question. What the person is really asking is, "How do I discover what *my* purpose is? And can you help me?" Essentially, they want to know how do I know what my "it" thing is? Of course it's a valid question. Yet many people already know the answer. They are just looking for the validation and a fool-proof, money-back guarantee that if they leave their comfort zone, then everything will work out.

Is Purpose Overrated?

I recently did a Google search for "what is your purpose." I wasn't surprised that there were over one billion results! As of the writing of this book, there are over 320 million people in the United States, who have online access to billions of literature in the marketplace to help them find their purpose. Many may recall Pastor Rick Warren's, *The Purpose Driven Life*, which was published in 2002, and continues to sell millions of copies worldwide. Why is it so important? Why do millions never find it? I have come to realize that they never find it because they never allow it to be born or they allow it to die in the discovery process.

I believe the late pastor, Myles Munroe, said it best: "the wealthiest place on earth is a cemetery." He stated that buried in the cemetery are:

- Books that were never written
- Music we've never heard
- Paintings no one has ever seen
- Poetry never read
- Businesses that have never opened
- Awesome companies that never got started
- Inventions we've never used

"The goal of life is to die empty. Don't die old, die empty."
- DR. MYLES MUNROE

There are a number of books, inspirational messages, and scriptures to remind us that God uniquely created each of us, and has given us a purpose that He desires for us to carry out on Earth. Technically speaking, we should all be "Purpose-Seekers." I summon you to heed your own call to action and get out of the way of your purpose. No more excuses. I'm speaking directly to those of you who are:

1. **Comfortable** – People who are satisfied with life just the way it is. They may have other desires, but leaving from where they are is not

worth the risk. Their daily routine provides exactly what they need to sustain themselves and their family without rocking the boat.

2. **Curious** – People who have a "feeling" that there is more, but for them to go after it, they're not sure just what the "it" really looks like. These are the people who typically say that nothing comes to mind when they think about pursuing their passion, yet they are open to search for what it is.

3. **Cautious** – People who know what they are supposed to do next. However, they are waiting on the "perfect" timing and "perfect" set of circumstances to align in order to begin or continue walking in faith.

4. **Creative** – People who have so many ideas and talents that they often do not know where to start or focus. They walk around with a debilitating fear of picking the wrong thing. Many also have a feeling that they should blend all their gifts together, yet are not exactly sure how to do that in a succinct way.

All four people are looking for the same thing, the courage to pursue their purpose. Before I share key questions to help you live a more purposeful and purpose-filled life, I am compelled to demystify the term. Truthfully, as much as I love the word "purpose," I equally dislike it! Gasp! Did I just say that? Yes, I did!

> *"Being overwhelmed with the big picture*
> *... can hinder you from being in the picture at all."*

The whole concept of purpose can be energizing and fulfilling for some, but overwhelming and daunting for others. There is something mind-boggling about hearing someone talk about his or her "life's work," "life-long dream," and "ultimate purpose." It can be very intimidating to someone, who has no clue to what they are passionate about. In my workshops, I ask participants to write down the things they are passionate about and would commit to doing for the next few years. I have seen the perplexed looks of those trying to figure out the answers to this question dozens of times.

Here is where I love to help people take the next steps towards finding their purpose without all of the overwhelming feelings that can come with such a daunting word. "Purpose" is just as much an "in the moment" term as it is a "life-long" term. So, before your heart constricts at the thought of figuring out what it is you want to do for the rest of your life, let's first start by focusing on this moment, right here and right now!

In a conversation with Stephanie, a human resources colleague, we ended up talking about what was next in her career. Like most people in corporate roles, her company had undergone major changes. All of these changes led to her having several downsizing conversations throughout the day with people being separated from the company. As you can imagine, that got old pretty quick. She knew her time would be up as well. As I tried to figure out what she wanted to do next, I got the common "I don't know!" answer from her. I remember going through a training called, "Fierce Conversations," where we were taught to ask, "What would it be if you did know?" in these types of situations. So, I asked again.

As it turns out, she did know! Not only that, but she had already done all the necessary research to find out what it would take to become a music therapist. This was the same field that gained notoriety for helping Congresswoman Gabrielle Giffords, (D-AZ) to find her voice through singing after the 2011 Tucson shootings. This wasn't just a passing thought for her, it was her dream. She attended open houses at a local university to learn more, conducted informational interviews with people in the field, and even job-shadowed to widen her understanding of how to perform in the field.

Most of us are hesitant like Stephanie. Her music therapy idea seemed a little too far left field. Especially since it was such a big career change. For years she had been too gun-shy to pull the trigger. She was even more discouraged once her father overheard her talking about in a phone conversation and completely shut down the idea. The fact is, most of us know what we want to do next. However, because the idea seems so different from where we are or where we thought we were going, we bury it in the recesses of our thoughts and only share practical answers we think others will agree with, to make us look "sane." Stephanie knew what she wanted to do, however, she struggled with conversations in her mind like, "What if I don't like it?" "What if it doesn't work?" All she saw was a complete career shift, instead of the two-year collegiate journey. Fortunately, for Stephanie, she followed her dream and left behind her HR career and enrolled in one of the top music therapy programs in the country. We can't all "Be Like Mike," but we can all "Be Like Stephanie!"

Again, don't think of "purpose" as making a life-long decision. Instead, look at it as taking a purposeful step in the direction you know you're supposed to be headed. In Stephanie's case, it would require going back to school. Being overwhelmed with the big picture will always keep us from stepping into the picture at all.

The treasure hunt for your purpose is just as much about creating purpose-filled experiences today as it is about discovering a bigger existence that you envision for tomorrow. The whole essence of purpose, regardless of whether you are in search of your life-long calling or simply looking for more fulfilling experiences in your day-to-day life, is to not settle into a life of merely existing. Rather, you want to ensure that everything you do is either purposeful or purpose-filled. The quickest way to a mundane and routine life is to lose sight of why you ever started down the road you are on in the first place.

Learning this new perspective about purpose and destiny is simply freeing. It is especially freeing for anyone who knows there is something different for them and is trying to figure out his or her next step. This new viewpoint helps to simplify the overall process.

10 Questions to Help You Discover Your Purpose

1. What's Your Passion? What do you love to do on your downtime, but you have no idea how you could ever make it your full-time?

_____

_____

_____

_____

2. What's your sweet spot? What are the things that come naturally to you?

_____

_____

_____

_____

3. What gives you a buzz? What is the thing that you would do for free?

_____

_____

_____

_____

4. What would it be if you removed the boundaries you've placed on your life?

_____
_____
_____
_____

5. Where do you love to add value to others?

_____
_____
_____
_____

6. What problem do you solve?

_____
_____
_____
_____

7. What is it about your future that keeps you up at night?

_____
_____
_____
_____

8. What tasks don't you like?

_____
_____
_____

9. What could you focus on today to help you prepare for your passion tomorrow?

_____
_____
_____
_____

10. What are you willing to do outside of your comfort zone?

_____

_____

_____

_____

11. Bonus Question!
What do you regret not doing thus far in your life?

_____

_____

_____

_____

COURAGEOUS SPOTLIGHT

A large part of my drive is my faith. Another aspect of that drive that fuels my journey is that I have seen too many people take risks and leap from their career to their calling and succeed! These women are not just semi-successful, but are operating in an earth-shattering, industry-changing, life-altering kind of way. They are excelling in their ideas and dreams in ways many others would love to do.

Throughout this book, I will introduce you to a few of my friends. They have not only changed their lives, but also have changed their industry and the lives of others. You will notice common traits, characteristics, and strategies in all of their success stories. I trust that you will see yourself in one or more stories of these amazing women. I know that you have so much in common with them because God made all of us unique, fearfully and wonderfully made. He equipped us with gifts, talents, ideas and witty inventions that He desires for us to fulfill.

Like you, all of the women featured in the ***Courageous Spotlight*** were sitting by the edge of the pool on the verge of a breakthrough. They finally heeded the call and leaped into their purpose. Below is the first snippet of an in-depth interview with a true courageous woman. To read the full interview, visit my website at courageouslifeacademy.com.

COURAGEOUS SPOTLIGHT

DANCING TO A DIFFERENT TUNE

Meet Courageous Jenni Catron
Author, Speaker and Leadership Expert

M: Jenni, take us back to your beginning and tell us how you started off in the music industry in Nashville, TN.

J: I was born and raised in northern Wisconsin, and as a little girl I fell in love with all things music. But something in my little girl heart knew I wasn't destined to be a great performer. I fear I might have been one of those children people say, "Why didn't anybody tell her she couldn't sing?" But I think God just put a little nugget in my heart and I realized what I wanted to do, even though I loved music, singing, and playing, I wanted to help artists accomplish their dreams. I remember being 13-years-old, figuring out as I looked at the back of CDs, that there were businesses that helped market and promote artists. Specifically for me, it was in the Christian music world. I wanted to help artists who were doing creative, thoughtful, Christian music, take it to the masses. At 13-years old I said, "I want to work at ForeFront Records in Nashville, TN for a living." When I graduated high school, I went to college in Tennessee and eventually got an internship at ForeFront Records and worked there for nine years.

M: When you and I connected, I knew you as this amazing church leader who was coming out with a new book called Clout. Tell us about the transition and the pivot you took from the music industry to church leadership.

J: That was a really fascinating journey for me. A journey of faith, because it was a place where I had this dream of being a music business executive since I was a kid. God had given me the opportunity to live that dream. I was racing up the corporate ladder and was a seat away from the executives wing. It was exactly the track I wanted to be on, but I began to get restless. I began to sense that I wasn't in the right seat. Maybe God had something else for me.

At the same time, my husband and I were part of a young church plant in Nashville, called Cross Point Church. The church was growing pretty rapidly, and Pete Wilson, the lead pastor there, would occasionally make a comment to me and say, "Hey, if you ever leave the music business, you should come and talk to me. Come and work for us." I *thought, "You're crazy. I've always wanted to work in the music business. This is my* dream job!" What would I do at a church? I'm a business major, I've been doing marketing and branding for nine years. But as that restlessness continued to grow in me, his comments kept ringing in my ears. I eventually took him to lunch and said, "Pete, what is this? What would I do here?"

The church was growing quickly and he needed somebody to come alongside him to help lead the staff and manage the organizational leadership. To oversee the day-to-day management that comes with operating a team in an organization. I had a friend from the music business say, when I announced I was leaving and going to work at this church, "Jenni, you're committing career suicide. What are you doing? You're on this trajectory to be an executive and you're going to go work at some little, unknown church? That's crazy." But there was such a sense of peace that it was God's calling that was unexplainable.

M: Such a step of faith! There are so many people who feel, "I may not be in the right seat." You made the leap and now you are thriving and applying your gifts at this church plant in Nashville, TN. While you were there you came out with the book Clout: *Discover and Unleash Your God-Given Influence. Tell us how the concept came about?*

J: As a kid, I loved writing. I was always interested in the creative arts. I dreamed of writing a book, but you grow up and say, "That's an audacious dream. Push out that one, because that's only for certain people." When I was at Cross Point, as the church was growing, I discovered I needed more outlets to communicate my heart and vision for what we were doing as an organization with the congregation. What's beautiful about Clout was it was my personal processing of the journey God had taken me on as a leader so far. The subtitle is, "Discover and Unleash Your God-Given Influence." Leadership begins with influence. It begins with recognition of the influence we have and the lives of the people around us. I think sometimes we can be quick to jump ahead and want this audience over there. The thing God was teaching me about in my own life was my influence started with where I was and who was around me right now. Starting with family, friends, coworkers, and the staff I was leading.

M: I love it! One of the key things I hear from you is to start from where you are and lead with authenticity.

J: Yes! I feel this, even now, that temptation to get worried about everybody out there, instead of being faithful to what is right here, right now. I think that's a tension we as leaders wrestle with, because part of being a leader is seeing the future and wanting to work toward that. It is a tension we have to live in and be a good steward of what God has for us right now and build on that. I love your point about the authenticity piece. Frankly, that can be hard for me, because I like to look like I have everything all together.

M: People need to see people like yourself, me or whomever that are real about what's happening in life, ministry, and leadership.

J: I think as leaders – I call it the "leadership sandwich". My job is to be in the middle of that, or sometimes I'll picture an Oreo cookie because that's my favorite! My job is to be the middle and I have somebody who is influencing me on one side and somebody who I'm pouring into and influencing on the other. If we ever think we are to the pinnacle, where we're pouring into others and there's nobody pouring into us, it's a really dangerous place to be. Processing and leading through the authenticity of real life is valuable to our peers and to the people who are learning from us.

M: What I'd love for you to share is what would you say to the person that's feeling, "I may not be in the right seat and this is what I've wanted to do my entire life." How would you encourage them today?

J: I would first say, God doesn't waste anything. While I was first confused about that kind of radical turn in my career and thinking, "God, did I just miss you in doing this thing or am I really hearing you with this other thing?" You're not crazy! God takes the most unique experiences and works all things together for good. Even if it feels like a crazy turn or you wonder, "did I miss you before this?" Probably not. It's really fascinating to see how God will use different elements of our story and weave them together. I would also say, slow down, be prayerful, and faithful to the next step. Those are my major leads. I always want to know what I'm supposed to do; I think we're all wired that way. I want it to be clear and I'll just do it. And it's never that way. The process is always slower and a little fuzzier than I really want it to be. When I was moving from the music business to Cross Point Church, I would wake up and say, "Okay, God, what's my step for today?" God is always faithful. If I try to run ahead, I usually start running in the wrong direction. Patient persistent progress is something God continues to remind me of. I'll feel urgency for movement and I think being more reconciled is a slow, steady progress. Be faithful for whatever that is for today and leaving tomorrow to tomorrow.

M: That is exactly what people need to hear Jenni. Thank You.

Can you believe Jenni left her dream job of working at a record company? She was one foot away from the executive office, and she chose to lead in ministry. Jenni is currently operating on another level that would have not been possible in her prior career. Jenni took a leap that changed the entire trajectory of her career. The type of career change that is possible for you too. This type of change only happens when you are open to doing what is right for you versus what is right according to others.

WALKING OUT STEP #1

"For I know the plans I have for you," declares the LORD,
*"**plans** to prosper you and not to harm you,*
* **plans** to give you hope and a future."*
- JEREMIAH 29:11

Most people walk around with this nagging dilemma, wondering what's next? The only way to ever find out is to commit to intentionally exploring all the angles and then walking it out. After you think about the questions you answered regarding your purpose, take some time to reflect. Do you notice any common themes when you look at your responses? Some of you will have a eureka moment that will give you the energy and momentum you need to take the next step. Others may get frustrated because they still don't have an answer. Being uncertain is not as bad as it seems. However, not putting in the ongoing work, reflection, and prayer until you find out is the key. A huge part of each courageous step is trusting and knowing that God has a plan for EVERYONE, even you!

Prayer for my Purpose & Vision

_____

_____

_____

_____

_____

_____

_____

_____

_____

_____

COURAGEOUS STEP #2

CAN I DO THIS?

*"I would rather run with my dream and trust in
Him, than to sit and wait for approval or affirmation
from others, while wallowing in my fears."*

Now that you have taken some time to dive deeper into what is next for you, let's take a look at what it takes to get there. I know you've thought about it, maybe you have even seen a vision like I did when I was in high school. Better yet, how many times have you worked on something and people complimented you about your gifts? However, for some reason, you are still stagnant. I am convinced that what holds people back from going after their dreams is not that they lack knowledge of what their calling is, rather what steps are required to fulfill it.

*"For everyone to whom much is given,
from him much will be required."*
- LUKE 12:48

I'm pretty sure many of you have thoughts of, "Can I disrupt what I have now, for something I don't know for sure will work out?" or "Why would I go from having it all, to risking it all?" None of these are conversations and decisions that should be taken lightly. Just remember to keep an open-mind and be flexible if opportunities arise that could be advantageous to helping you make the next move.

I recall one calm winter night, lying in the middle of my living room floor crying out to God because I felt so inadequate compared to my dreams. Feelings of loneliness swept over me on days I felt misunderstood. It was like I did not fit in with everyone else. It seemed as if the rest of the world was comfortable living normal lives. All the while, I wrestled with the discomfort and monotony of my outwardly successful life. I remember those feelings of fear all too well. Thinking to myself, *will this career move really work out for me?* There were so many more questions and surges of apprehension going on in my mind.

What fuels and propels me is that I refuse to believe in a God that will not do for me what He has done for others, like the women highlighted in this book, and the countless courageous women past and present. There is absolutely no way – it's not possible. So, I would rather run with my dream and trust in Him, than to sit and wait for approval or affirmation from others, while wallowing in my fears.

You Are What You Think

"Finally, brethren, whatsoever things are true,
whatsoever things are honest, whatsoever things are just,
whatsoever things are pure, whatsoever things are
lovely, whatsoever things are of good report;
if there be any virtue, and if there be any praise,
think on these things."
- PHILIPPIANS 4:8

I have mentioned to you that this process is filled with so many thoughts and emotions. Some are invigorating, a number of them defeating. I remember this short Bible verse since I was a little girl that says, "The enemy comes to steal, kill, and destroy."(John 10:10). That basically means, "It isn't going to be easy, honey!"

How many of you are like me? As soon as I get excited and see a little bit of traction, opposition starts to rise up out of nowhere. To the point where it literally feels like the devil is sitting on my shoulder trash-talking, saying things like:

"Who do you think you are?"
"You don't have enough money!"
"You don't know enough people!"
"Your idea is crazy! In fact, you're crazy!"

"People aren't going to support you!"
"No one knows you!"
"Look where you come from!"
"Remember the mistakes you've made?"
"You didn't even go to school."

Ugh! I can keep going on, but I won't, because you have probably been doing a good job of compiling and rehearsing your own list. Don't worry. I have, too, but I have learned to lean on my faith more than any emotion I feel.

Do you realize that whatever your day-to-day thoughts are, eventually become your reality? One of my favorite scriptures states,

"These things I have spoken to you, that in Me you may have peace. In the world you will have tribulation; but be of good cheer, I have overcome the world."
- JOHN 16:33

How GREAT is that? It's major! Do you know that this passage refers to all the negative thoughts that keep being thrown at you? The ones that as soon as you get rid of it, another one takes its place. Every time you start having these crazy conversations of obstacles and excuses to pursue your dreams, don't believe them. The devil is waiting to snatch the very innovative ideas that God has given you out of your head, your heart, and your mouth. Once you begin to master your nagging thoughts, and meditate on this scripture, life begins to change. You will eventually get a little swagger in your step and your confidence grows. It not only says that you've got this, but you've got this, NOW!

I am thankful that right before launching my business, God revealed to me several key things I needed to know that have launched my journey:

Realization #1 – God Was Waiting On Me
Have you ever had an experience that was completely life-changing, eye-opening, and awakened something inside you? Maybe it was something you did, heard, or saw with your own eyes?

For me it was something I heard. I will never forget listening to my pastor speaking about Joshua 3:13, one Sunday:

> *"It shall come about when the soles of the feet of the*
> *priests who carry the ark of the Lord, the Lord of all*
> *the earth, rest in the waters of the Jordan, the waters*
> *of the Jordan will be cut off, and the waters which are*
> *flowing down from above will stand in one heap."*

Now, I cannot tell you for the life of me what my pastor was preaching about at that moment. Instead, I do know this scripture sounded like someone had literally just dropped my favorite Mikasa dish in the kitchen. BOOM! It struck me so hard!

Although, I felt strongly about what was next for me, I had started, stopped, and stalled for years. Then I heard that scripture. It was on that day, I knew my destiny depended on me! I could not wait to be discovered, as I sometimes secretly hoped. Even though I had a gift for speaking, I had to secretly stop wishing that someone would ask me to come speak at a workshop or Conference.

As I heard the scripture and mulled on it over and over again, I realized **I had to take the first step.** It was not that my original plan was not going to work, it was just that my plan was waiting on ME to work IT! When I started walking in the direction of my dreams, the path was cleared for me, just as it said in the above passage. I started hosting mini-retreats for my friends and coaching them. People's lives were being changed because of ME!

Realization #2 - It's a Win-Win

My dad was always an advocate for education, especially my education. He constantly told me that education is the one thing people cannot take from you. I remember sitting in my office, caught up in the familiar matrix of thinking, planning, and praying for my vision. But for some reason, on that day, this time it was different. I experienced a revelation that gave me the confirmation to step out on faith. Suddenly, I clearly heard my dad's voice reminding me that I already received my education so no one could take it away! Besides, it hit me that if I ever felt like I wanted to (or even needed to) go back to Corporate America, I could. Although I have no plans on returning, that day and that conversation was exactly what I needed to transition me from sitting behind a desk that I didn't own, to setting up my own home office.

Realization #3 – There is an Audience for You

On that same day in my office, I finally made up my mind to move forward. I saw a vision of me in a room full of people that provided exactly the same services as I dreamed. They were speakers, trainers, coaches, and more. We were all standing upfront to showcase our gifts and talents. All of us had very similar styles, props, and topics. Talk about intimidating! I thought, *The market is saturated and everyone is great, how in the world am I going to make myself stand out?* As my vision progressed, I finished talking and I saw a light shine on a portion of the audience that was specifically drawn to ME! In an overcrowded room where it sounded like everyone was saying the same thing, I realized there was a specific audience just for me. They were drawn to *MY* voice and *MY* message, no one else's. It was these three revelations that caused me to realize not only could I do this, but I could do this today.

Mindset Mastery

"We all have recurring negative thoughts. Just don't get stuck there."

I got to the point in my faith-walk where I knew I had to control and monitor my thoughts if I was going to proceed full speed ahead. However, I had yet to be introduced to terms like mindset mastery. Some of you are probably saying, "Yes, me too!" Others may be saying, "What in the world is that?" Once I learned, I said "Oh yeah, I'll take a supersize of that please!" Mindset Mastery is the power of reflecting, meditating, and believing the truth about ourselves and our futures.

Of course, there is much more to this concept, but people don't make the leap from their career to their calling because they never master the art of overcoming what plagues them the most, their thoughts. They end up succumbing to the negative thoughts, voices, and emotions in their hearts or heads which constantly say, "No, you can't."

I have had to learn and practice mindset mastery each day. Most days, it is moment-by-moment. If I gave in to those nagging feelings in the back of my mind, I would never have been able to write this book. For example, a very real thought I often battled with as I began to express my thoughts on paper was, "Why in the *world are you doing all this work? No one is going to read it anyway!*" Imagine, if I listened to, reflected on, and meditated on that every day? Guess what? There would be NO book, because I would have eventually talked myself out of writing It.

Like myself, you need to let go of the thoughts of failure. Think about the questions below as you change your mindset and walk out Step 2.

1. What aspects of your journey concern or frighten you if you say "Yes"?

_____

_____

_____

_____

2. What have you talked yourself out of doing that could move you closer to your dream? Think about those missed opportunities recently or in the past.

_____

_____

_____

_____

3. What mistruths can you now give up as you practice meditating and reflecting on your positive future?

_____

_____

_____

_____

COURAGEOUS SPOTLIGHT

SOARING BEYOND BOUNDARIES

Meet Courageous Elizabeth McCormick ~ Black Hawk pilot Keynote Speaker, Author of The Pilot Method

M: Tell us about your current role.

E: I am a motivational speaker, leadership trainer, and I travel all over the world. I have about 120 engagements a year and I write books. I do a little bit of mentoring, but I like to be on those big stages.

M: Prior to you becoming a world-renowned keynote speaker, you also had a pretty interesting military career. Tell us about how you became a Black Hawk pilot.

E: I was an unemployed military wife. I had just finished college with a couple degrees. We were stationed in Ft. Polk, LA, where there's not even a Wal-Mart. It was a big swampland. There's a lot more there now than when I was there.

I was miserable. One night, I'm laying there awake, turned, and looked at – I call him my "starter husband" – the back of his head and thought, "You know what? If he can be in the Army, why can't I? I can do this." I decided I was going to move, take action, and do something different. I believe we all have potential inside of us to be more than what we currently are. We have to make a decision, commit to that decision, and then take action on that decision. I researched it and decided the coolest job was being a helicopter pilot. I was 23 and I wanted the coolest job. I went to talk to the pilots and had that aha moment when I looked at the helicopters for the first time. I had that vision that this was what I was supposed to do. I saw it! I saw myself out there on that flight line, with those helicopters, wearing a flight suit that actually still fits thanks to Spanx! I researched it and asked around. I said, "What do I need to do?" And people helped me until I went to the recruiter and then they weren't so helpful. The recruiter told me, "You can't do that."

M: How did you respond?

E: When someone tells you you can't do something, it's time to get curious and ask, "Why not? As adults, where has our curiosity gone? Be curious and find out what is standing in your way! Sometimes it could be something simple. Sometimes there's a law standing in your way. There's a law, there's rules – those can get changed! If you believe enough, if you're willing to work hard enough, willing to fight the fight to make that change. If I had not walked into that recruiting station and questioned him – someone who should have known their job – I would have never become a helicopter pilot. My entire world and life changed because I was willing to believe in my potential of what I could be, more than I was willing to believe in someone else's limiting beliefs.

M: That is very powerful. I love that you said you didn't have to know the "how." You didn't have to know the end before the beginning.

E: Flying a helicopter is not like anything else. It would be like riding a roller coaster where you're in the front car. You see everything, you feel everything, and you get to decide where it goes. How high, how low, how fast, or how slow, to the right or to the left. It's an amazing experience to be the pilot of a machine of such magnitude. And it's a little intimidating. I must admit, when I first started, I was the only female in my class.

Not just my class, but I was one of the few female pilots. I was so intimidated by everything going on around me. The helicopter and the unit. When you're in those situations and feel like you're out of your league, sometimes the best thing to do is to become a really good observer. I sat back, watched what everybody else did, and tried to fit in. I had to create my own curriculum in life and make it happen.

M: Observation and creating your own path, in order to make it happen. How long did you do it and what caused the transition?

E: I was stationed over in Germany and I was injured. I received some bad medical care and I would never fly again. So, I went on this web site called Monster.com. It was brand new back then! I got a job. I had an interview within three days of leaving Germany and got the job. I worked in the company for five years. I had my head down and didn't even consider speaking. I didn't consider utilizing any of those skills or stories. I didn't document or journal. I was wounded, not just physically, but emotionally after losing my career. I had been stalked and physically abused by another pilot for eight months and my chain of command let that happen. So, for me, I needed to heal. Sometimes we just need to excuse ourselves and give ourselves a break. I didn't realize that was what I was doing at the time.

I was a single parent. I had my head down and checked in and out. I did what I needed to do, and gave myself some space and time to heal. If I had been more self-aware, I probably should have been in therapy, but you didn't do that. I worked for three different companies over the span of about eight years, and I did my job. In year six, I woke up. I said, "Whoa, there's a light bulb here!" I was remarried – this is the "keeper" husband.

I was interviewed for Veteran's Day for the local newspaper and an article went out. From that article, I got asked to start speaking. I started speaking for youth groups and church groups and they were calling me, but I was working a job! I started turning them down and they started offering me money. I went, "Oh, okay. That's interesting. Around that same time, the corporation I was working for laid off the entire division.

Over 200 people were laid off and I was one of those 200 people. Shortly after that, I was working with a network marketing company and they, within two weeks of me being out of that job, called me and asked me to come on the road with them and travel as a trainer. I started speaking for the network marketing company and traveled to do motivational leadership and sales training. After about a year, they pulled me aside and said, "We love you. The audience loves you, but they want to know more about your helicopter pilot stories than our company stories. We just think you have something bigger than us."

Shortly after that, they didn't renew my contract. It gave me the confidence to go solo and represent myself. No contract, just represent myself, work my business, and become a professional. I drew the line in the sand and said, "I am now a professional speaker, this is what I'm going to do full-time." I invested my retirement 401k into myself. I invested in me and my future. It's a non-stop marketing machine to be a professional speaker. You're constantly, "What's next? What content is next? What speech is next? What next video can you shoot?" It's a constant push.

Every day that I'm not putting myself out there, not pushing, not doing what I know I need to do, I am getting in my own way. There's somebody out there that's not getting what they need, because I know my message helps people to make a difference. I'm wondering how many of us have something. A service, a product, a vision, a plan for something that's going to help somebody else. Every day you're in your way on that, you're keeping someone away from something that could change their life. How dare you withhold that from them? Because you're scared. Or you don't know. Or you're not sure. Get out of your own way and amazing things happen.

M: What would you tell the person sitting in an unfulfilling career?

E: If it's not you, then who? If you have something within you, a vision, a dream, an idea, our responsibility is to move that into reality. Why would we mess that up? It comes right back to our job being not to get in our way of our own potential. It's to fulfill it. What happens is that we listen to everyone else's limiting beliefs. My dad told me, "You can't make a living as a speaker. What are you kidding?" My own dad!

M: I need to pause right there, because there is somebody who has a family member, parent, spouse, or sibling that is feeding those negative thoughts. How did you even overcome that? How do you overcome your loved one saying, "You can't do that?"

E: Prove them wrong! Choose to believe in yourself more than them. How do they know? They're not in your head. They haven't had the vision. They haven't seen it. It doesn't matter if you describe it; it's not the same as what you have in you. Use it as fuel for your fire. Prove that you can do it. I've created a new program available to help you called F.L.Y. "First Lead Yourself," so you can be a better leader for others."

Elizabeth is a prime example of taking a courageous step to do something not only uncommon, but totally unfamiliar. Talk about stepping out of her comfort zone! Not only did she take action on her vision of becoming a Black Hawk helicopter pilot, she kicked the door down to the gender stereotypes. Elizabeth has proven to herself and the world that she can indeed, soar beyond boundaries. It's your turn to do whatever it takes. Stop asking whether you can do something. Just do it!

YOU ARE YOUR PRIORITY

Over time, we become great in the roles of superman or superwoman in our lives, our careers, and to our families. "Yes I can do that." "Yes, I can go there." "No that won't be a problem," and "Of course, that's fine." It starts to become a way of life, only to leave us continuously adding on more duties, while never letting go of the things that no longer fit who and where we are headed. Most of all, leaving no room for who we are to become.

Fully committing to your future self must be done by any means necessary. Therefore, you have to let some things go or renegotiate how they get done. Before you jump into full activation mode, I encourage you to pause in order to assess what needs to change or be recalibrated in your life.

Think through each of the following categories below and list some activities you need to start, stop, or continue for optimal effectiveness. The quickest way to get stuck and frustrated is to add more onto an already full schedule. Take a deeper look into what creating space for your God-given dreams looks like. Key areas to think about are:

- Family
- Career
- Community
- Social Life
- Finances

Creating space and saying yes to *you* means that you are going to have to say "no" to others. I know it's not the easiest thing to do. I have turned down going to the movies or out to dinner many times in pursuit of my transition to my calling. Remember, as you recalibrate your life and renegotiate your time, only the people who do not understand your vision will not understand the sacrifices you have to make. Everyone else will be elated that you have finally put a stake in the ground and created the necessary space to be your best self.

Eliminating Distractions

Social Media

Creating space is just as much about eliminating distractions as it is about making sacrifices. Social media became my addiction. Throughout the day I mindlessly scrolled through my Facebook, Twitter, and Instagram timelines, engrossed with other people's lives, when I should have been working on my own. For me, it was social media, for you it may be your favorite TV shows, browsing the Internet, online shopping, or being on the phone constantly. Whatever distractions you use to pass time, they have to be reevaluated, if not cut out altogether.

Phone

In college, I had friends who lived all over the country. After spending four years together in some of the craziest times of our life, it was obvious we needed to stay connected. I embarked upon a lifelong and intimate relationship with my phone, because I moved away from my family and close friends. My entrepreneurial buddies live all around the world, too. Talk about a bunch of low battery notifications, full voicemails, and me repeating "Can you hear me now?" as I drove through dead zones and country roads.

For years, my phone was my lifeline. However, it quickly turned into my biggest distraction when it came time for me to pursue my dreams. I was stalling. I continued my old habits while carrying a desire to create a new lifestyle. Whether it was the phone, social media, or my social life, I found that I encountered more bedtimes with nothing crossed off of my to-do list. For you, it might be family, school, or work. What is the thing that feels like it is always eating at your time? Only when we admit what is getting in our way, can we proactively work toward removing it.

WALKING OUT STEP #2

"If you are searching for peace, you will find it knowing that you are living in God's will, even when you are uncomfortable."

There are 4 Key Elements required to leap from your career to your calling:

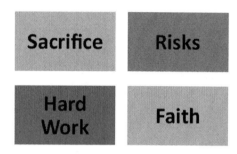

Sacrifice: You must be willing to give up something in order to make room for walking in your true calling.

Risk: Without risk-taking, you will remain in your comfort zone and miss advantageous unforeseen opportunities.

Hard Work: It all boils down to "how bad do you want it?" There are no shortcuts to success and no substitutes for hard work.

Faith: Scripture tells us that without faith, works is dead. You must apply your faith to God's word and allow Him to fulfill His promises to You.

Honestly, if you choose not to address that tug in your heart or the thoughts that keep you up at night, your life will still be good! Of course, you will have your great career, do all the amazing things that you do now, but eventually the tug will pull harder. Once you have the revelation of what God called you to do, then be willing to discover what it takes to bring it to life. I've learned that peace is not being comfortable. Peace is knowing that you are living in God's will even when you are uncomfortable.

Moving from your career to your calling can be the most exhilarating, exhausting, and exciting time in your life. Since you're on the journey now,

I'm sure you know what I mean. Keep moving forward. Your step was only meant for you!

COURAGEOUS STEP #3

DO YOU BELIEVE GOD?

"One of the most dangerous people in the world is a
dreamer who does not believe!"

The spring of 2013 changed my life forever! That spring, I was hosting my family visiting from Virginia. A highlight on the itinerary was a trip to one of our local attractions in Charlotte – the Billy Graham Library, a tour and tribute in honor of the well-known pastor. It was also my first time, so I did not know what to expect, fortunately God knew what I needed.

There was one part of the tour where they showed an old clip of Billy Graham being interviewed on the Phil Donahue Show. In that short segment, Phil asked Pastor Graham specific questions about the Bible. He asked one, then another, and then another. All I can remember was Pastor Graham saying, "That's just it Phil, you can't explain it, you just have to believe!"

I remember God speaking to me in that moment. If I wanted to stop all of my emotional ups and downs, all the false starts, all the inconsistencies in my joy, then I would have to tackle the root of the issue; my lack of belief. My disbelief in the fact that I had a great future ahead of me outside of a bi-weekly corporate paycheck. My doubt that I would ever get married. My lack of faith that I could actually leap from my career to my calling. I left that tour with the biggest revelation that transformed my entire mindset.

There was a time when I was so tired in my spirit, and my emotions were all over the place. It seemed like I was touchy and finicky about everything; my coffee was too cold, there was too much traffic, or the waitress forgot extra napkins. While there was nothing radically wrong, it felt like I could go from laughing to crying or joy to depression in two seconds flat. More importantly, I grew tired of feeling great in church during praise and worship and hearing an awesome message, but going home and instantly feeling defeated again. For some reason, I believed God's word for everyone else, but not for me. I constantly asked myself, "What in the world is wrong with me?" I couldn't figure it out and nothing made sense.

Don't get me wrong, I love church. But what I found out during that season, and continue to learn daily, is that attending church without intentionally believing God's word, is just a weekly routine with no real transformation. Who has time for that? I didn't! I could have been traveling, shopping, or spending time with friends and family. I had to rethink my whole Sunday regimen. Why continue to show up, if I did not believe in myself nor believe the God that I said I loved and served? I was fed up with tradition. I needed change.

Can you relate to my story? Maybe your story does not include church at all, but it does include strong feelings of needing change or dealing with a lack of belief.   It possibly even includes believing there are big things ahead for someone else, but you never thought about yourself with that same level of assurance. Chances are if you did, it was probably short-lived.

Make Your Mark

"Whatever you want in life, other people are going
to want it too. Believe in yourself enough to accept
the idea that you have an equal right to it."
- DIANE SAWYER

Moving from your career to your calling is not about being the next big celebrity in your industry. In my case, it is not about being the next Oprah, Brene Brown, or Joyce Meyer. Instead, it is about becoming the very best at what God created me to do. Somewhere between our childhood dreams and planning for retirement, we lose the one thing required to get us there – VISION. Vision for our life, vision for our future, and vision for our families. Our vision of what could be possible, quickly changes into an unfulfilled habit of running from one thing to the next. Our narrow focus of the day-to-day leaves little room to see no further than what is directly in front of us.

I imagine you can think back to the time when you told yourself, "I will only be at this job for a few years, then I will pursue my dreams." To your surprise, that was 20 New Year's Eve celebrations ago! Then again, maybe you are the one who said, "I'll go back to school in a year." It's 10 years later and your youngest child is in college on Spring Break. Is it time for you to dust off that half-written business plan you wrote a few years ago? The one you recently found tucked away after purging your home office. For many of us, it is "that thing" that God continues to gently tug at our heart about starting, restarting, or not giving up on.

That was me for several years. I cannot tell you the countless conversations I had with my friends about speaking, teaching, and training. The numerous false starts I had. The coaches I hired. The classes I attended. It was not that I lacked a vision. It was not that I could not figure out how to believe in myself to get it done. Yes, I had a lot to learn, but I had not yet bought into my vision nor increased my faith in God to believe that it could work.

> *"We may encounter many defeats but we must not be defeated."*
> *- DR. MAYA ANGELOU*

Wrestling with my lack of belief in what God could do in my life, was the catalyst that enabled me to restart this journey for the last time. It is what enables me to keep going on my darkest day, when my emotions say, "This is not working, give up now." You have to get to a point in your life where you believe that God will do what He says for YOU. The moment when your decisions are no longer based on what YOU know, what YOU see, and what YOU can do, are the moments when God can step in and do only what He can do!

I wish I could I tell you that once you understand and go through the dark days, you will not have to deal with them anymore. That once you wrestle with it and allow your heart to be transformed, your lack of belief will be cured forever. Sorry. I honestly, still wrestle with doubt. In every moment, I have to CHOOSE to believe how big God is and how small I am. No matter what I see or don't see, it does not mean God has not made a way for opportunity and provision. He has and He always will.

> *Be anxious for nothing, but in everything by prayer*
> *and supplication, with thanksgiving, let your*
> *requests be made known to God; 7 and the peace of*

God, which surpasses all understanding, will guard
your hearts and minds through Christ Jesus.
PHILIPPIANS 4:6-8 (NKJV)

Confidence vs. Courage

"The difference between courage and confidence is faith!"

A good friend once asked me what the difference was between confidence and courage. She said that she is often courageous and acts upon what she is expected to do, but most times lacks confidence. She added, "I'll show up to a meeting or networking event that I feel is required of me, but I don't feel like I am supposed to be there. Sometimes I don't know what I'm supposed to say." I told her that she needed to increase her faith in God's word. Faith comes by hearing the word of God (Romans 1:17). I believe that the difference between courage and confidence is faith.

We think, plan, and pray about our goals because we are looking for a fool-proof, money-back guaranteed plan. We are waiting until we feel super confident, not only in our own ability, but also in the eventual outcome. When you are doing something that is beyond your comfort zone, you will never feel confident. At least, not to the degree that you feel comfortable. The space between where you are and where you want to be is simply faith. The only way to get to where you want to go, is to take one step of faith at time.

You can read the rest of this book and create a plan that helps you to fulfill the very call of God on your life. However, there will never be a plan, seminar, or coach that can substitute the only thing that you can ever produce yourself: BELIEF. It is the essence, the foundation, and the engine of the very thing you feel like you are supposed to do in your life.

The fulfillment of God's call on your life comes from the vision He placed inside of you. Coupled with your belief that He can do it through you, and your following through with the plan. If you miss any one of these components, you may feel stuck, frustrated, and unfulfilled. The reason we were created cannot be boiled down to a formula or oversimplified with a few "feel good" words. However, having the quick ability to see what's missing, helps to determine where to focus, so we can move forward with momentum.

COURAGEOUS SPOTLIGHT

FINE-TUNING A LIFE OF PURPOSE

**Meet Courageous Jade Simmons
World renowned classical pianist, Powerhouse
Speaker, Bestselling Author, Audacious Prayers**

M: You are a classical pianist. You have been able to play in some of the most beautiful places and play some of the most beautiful pieces of work that have literally set you apart from others. Tell us how you got started?

J: I started like most musicians start, with piano lessons. The big difference was I started really late. I didn't start taking official lessons until I was eight years old. The good thing about starting late was I had already heard tons of amazing music, including classical music. I came to the table with strong feelings about how I wanted to interpret music. What set me apart early was I was a passionate player when I was a little girl. I moved a lot, which didn't always score well in the competitions. I loved playing fast music and I had a penchant for rhythmic music, which, years later, would establish my career. I knew, by the time I was about 12, that this was what I wanted to do. I was very fortunate to have parents that said, "Pursue it!

M: Most parents tell their children, "You can do that, but make sure you do something that provides security as well, so you have a backup plan.

J: Of course! In their defense, I don't blame them, because it's a very difficult career to make it in the world of the arts. They're speaking from a place of good intentions, but it's usually a big mindset block to making it work.

M: What gave you the courage to say, "I get what the history of classical piano is like, but there's something different I want to do."

J: Let me be candid and say that my original vision was simply to be one of the world's most noted, black female concert pianists. All I wanted to do was play Beethoven, Bach, and Rachmaninoff. I wanted to wear my designer gowns, come out and play with the New York Philharmonic, and play purely classical music. That's the only definition I knew of what it meant to be a concert pianist. What's so awesome about reinvention is that the best reinvention is organic. It's not something you necessarily decide to create or make a gimmick around. What happened was I held this original vision, got out into the world, and realized all of the other classical pianists were going after the same thing. We were playing the same music, the same way we'd been taught, we'd been kind of secretly told to keep our personalities at bay. I was realizing that while I was making a decent career at it, I was trying to stand out by competing. As much as I love competition, this was a slow, dying way to build a career. It is why most emerging artists never emerge! They end up drowning. After I got tired of trying to compete by playing and doing the same things everyone else was doing, I started telling stories in between all of this big, fast playing to give myself a break between pieces. Lo and behold, the stories were making my concert! People started coming to hear me play, but also to hear the stories I was telling. Over the last five to eight years, I started introducing more modern classical music. Then I got very bold and started introducing some improvisation and electronics. Then, where I am today, from Rachmaninoff to rap! But it was an organic process of me simply saying, "Can I dare to be just a little bit more of me?"

You mentioned the risk. The risk was, "Am I going to scare off classical music connoisseurs?" Well, of course I am! "Am I going to scare off traditionalists?" Maybe so. But what happened was that my audiences began to be some of the most colorful and most diverse in terms of age and socioeconomic background in the world of classical music. By reinventing myself in that way, I began to reinvent the audience that came to hear classical music. I'm very proud of that.

M: There are two things you said in reference to reinvention – often it's not forced, it's organic. You also referenced competition. You realized that you were trying to stand out by competing, instead of trying to stand out by being who you are. Say more about those two things.

J: The best visual I can give, and I do this now with consulting clients who say, "I have this creative baby I want to birth. This is what I envision it's going to be and this is the color of the logo and..." I say, "Let's go back to purpose. A place of purpose and a place of mission." The big epiphany for me when you talk about competing was I was playing these concerts to impress people. I think subconsciously, being the lone, black female in the world of classical music, it felt like – of course I wasn't the only one, but it always felt like I was the only one. I had this subconscious pressure that I had to be extra classical, whatever that meant.

What I do now in my career is I only compare notes with my former self. I say, "What did Jade do last year? What was the big breakthrough last season? What is there still yet to be done? What is the corner I have not explored that would be organic to me?" The reason that reinvention scares everybody is because we imagine going into a big lab and having them mix up all these foreign chemicals. Really, reinvention is a process of peeling back the onion so you get to deeper layers of yourself. You're deciding, "Okay. I'm now going to put this part of myself on display, as well." It's going to look like something brand new to the audience, but for me it's going to feel like a version I haven't shared, or one I am also discovering about myself.

M: The one thing I know is that you are a quick start. How were you able to have the patience to go through this organic process?

J: First of all, I am an impatient person by nature. I want everything to happen yesterday. Literally, during college, I had a year where I prayed for patience every day. I wanted to be more patient with people, more patient with myself, because as a quick start, you want everybody to quick start. "Why are you moving so slow?" Even though I can talk to you now about this organic process, when it was happening, a lot of it was me throwing gum on the wall and seeing if it would stick! I was trying things out. "Is the audience going to like this? This feels good to me. Let's see what works. Okay, this worked, this didn't. Which one of these things feels more organic?" I was still operating as a quick start. I had to learn to step back and say, "What is working?" And then decide which part, of all the things I was quick starting worked and made sense. Multi-talented creatives, can get in a rut of only launching stuff and being moved by their emotion and what they want to do. Having the courage to say, "Gosh darn it, I'm going to stick with this one thing for at least two months," which is like hell.

M: Not too long after you said, "You know what? I am going to step out and be even more of who God has called me to be. Then, next thing you know, here comes what is a legacy devotional that people will read and be blessed beyond your generation, Audacious Prayers. Talk to us about taking on yet another aspect of reinvention.

J: What I'm going to say to you is what I wish someone told me when I was younger. I've always been that typical American, over-achiever kid, who did 50 million different activities all at once. I played three sports, I was class president every year, student body president senior year, marching band, youth symphony – you name it, I did all of it. I remember one of my band teachers, he would call me "Jadey!", he would say, "Jade, one day the people in the white jackets are going to come get you!" Can you imagine me being in a straight jacket by the time I was 30? People with multiple gifts make the mistake of doing everything we can do, versus focusing on the things we must do and are designed to. Now I am learning to prioritize all of my activities by purpose. If it's writing a book that gives us the big, bold words to match our big, bold dreams. Does that line up? Yep, it's pushing people, I can do it. If it's hosting a broadcast for a classical music show, am I going to host it in a way that pushes people to see the music differently, or to learn about these artists differently? If it involves pushing, I can do it. But God has these seasons where he says, "Now I'm going to put you out front and you're going to be primarily doing what I originally designed you to do." That's the season I'm in now and it feels okay. I don't have to explain why the classical pianist is writing a book about prayer. Because I know when I play a concert, it's going to push you. When I write a book, it's going to push you. When I speak, it's going to push you. It's going to push you toward purpose and it's also going to ultimately push you toward more passionate pursuit of God and a divinely aligned life.

M: Can you tell us about Audacious Prayers, how it even came about and whom it's for?

J: I'm still blown away by how the book has taken off. Sometimes God will wake me up and say, "I want you to do this." I wrote this devotional two years ago, over this span of two days over Christmas break. And I promptly sat on it. I didn't know what to do with it, I didn't feel led to release it, I just knew I needed to write it. I was so steeped at that point; I was at the height of doing all of my classical music stuff that it made no common branding or marketing sense for me to put out a book on prayer. It's so wonderful how his timing is so much better than ours. I ended up meeting a guy named Dr. Fred Jones, who is a publishing strategist. After about six months of knowing each other, I was talking to him about books I had on my heart. I said, "I've got 20 book ideas on a given day. Listen to these top five and tell me what you think. He said, "Which one is ready to go?" And I said, "The prayer book is pretty much written." He said, "You need to go with that." I said, "Are you sure? I don't know how to market." He said, "Prayer is universal. Everybody needs prayer." So, we launched it. Thinking I was doing things sort of randomly, I had no idea that the release date would coincide with the National Day of Prayer. I had no idea at the time that my pastor would ask me to speak on Mother's Day, which would be right before the National Day of Prayer. I had no idea at the time I would be leading up a women's seminar. All of a sudden, I was a minister releasing a book on prayer.

I went from being this concert pianist, who didn't know why she was writing about prayer, to being in the ministry releasing a book on prayer. It has been mind blowing, just because of the response. I'm so inspired by your commitment to courage and helping others be courageous. That's what this book is designed to do and I'm humbled to see the effect it's having on people's lives.

We have a God that has a great sense of humor and He loves surprises from what I can tell of His nature. I am noticing that He seems to love outdoing my so-called big dreams by dropping unexpected, bigger things in my lap. It's like he's training us to think bigger. That's what's exciting, because I believe it's going to open people's eyes to how small they've been living and how big the possibilities really are.

M: What about someone that is not a big risk taker who is saying, "I'm going to try these different things with my career and step out of the box." What would you tell that person?

J: Understand that reinvention comes from within. If you can understand that, all the things you need to do differently are already within you. All the tools, you're already equipped with them. You have the knowledge and skills you need. Reinvention begins from within. I would also say throw away the word 'reinvention'. Change it to 'reintroduction'. What you're doing is reintroducing yourself to you. Everything I'm doing now, even the new stuff that's ahead, I can find examples of me doing it from being a little girl. It's much less scary than thinking, "I have to now become something completely different than I already am." You're saying, "I am going to commit to becoming more of who I have always been." That will take a lot of the jitters out of the process.

Do you see areas where you can fine-tune and reinvent yourself? Your courageous step may be a lot easier than you think. Especially if you are like Jade where you have already put in the hard work, training in a particular field. How can you make a slight twist in your expertise marketable? How can you make it fun for yourself and others? Invoking a smile and laughter in a specialized field, is bound to make room for entirely new audiences and opportunities. It's not all black and white. Add your splash of color. Start practicing your happy dance and shake yourself out of the box!

The Calling

> **Definition:**
> *Calling* - A place beyond where I am
> that God has destined for me
> to be, thrive, and make an impact.

The transition that propelled me from my career to my calling took me on a personal journey of entrepreneurship. Many of you may feel the entrepreneurship bug, as well. However, moving into your calling is not just about starting a business, it's about being in the place that God has for you in this specific season of your life.

Most people associate having a "calling" with being church-related or going into official ministry. You may have heard someone say that about themselves or others say they have been "called" into the ministry. Which means that like you and I, there was this tugging on their heart that was so big they could no longer ignore it. The only option was to say "Yes!"

For many of us who feel this tug and know that they are "called" to do something more, it's more than a ministerial feeling. Most people fear public speaking anyway, so I doubt many of us have a desire to get up and preach a sermon. However, we all can definitely relate to the same agonizing and passionate tug in our hearts that says there is something more for us beyond where we are now.

That "something more" could be a new role, a new business, starting a ministry, or the decision to stay home with your family. It could even mean becoming a bigger, better, and bolder version of who you are today. It is essentially saying, "Yes God, I'll go" to the place you have designed for me to thrive, and make an impact!" It's the place that you feel drawn when you wake up in the morning.

Walking towards your calling does not mean that you have finally arrived. Nor does it mean things are finally going to be easy. In fact, you will experience moments of joy, discontentment, and so many other positive and negative emotions along the way. But unlike the season that you are leaving, this new season will be one filled with even greater purpose, impact, and fulfillment.

Walking in your calling is a "beyond you" experience. It is a time in your life where you finally say, "No!," to doing things based on your own skills, abilities, and what you can see. Instead, you begin to trust in what you do not see or have. You will begin to have increased faith and trust that God can help you achieve your goals and dreams. It is easy to say you have faith when you know you have another paycheck coming in two weeks. It is also easy to have faith when you can predict your day and already know what your future looks like. However, don't worry about what tomorrow holds. God knows.

WALKING OUT STEP #3

"Call to me and I will answer you and tell you great and unsearchable things you did not know."
- JEREMIAH 33:3

As you walk out this next step of believing that God has a perfect plan in store for you, keep reminding yourself of the vision He gave you for success. Your faith must be applied to His Word every day in order for you to execute the grand plan for your calling.

- **Vision** - I know what I want to do.
- **Belief** - I know that it can happen for me.
- **Execution** - I am taking consistent and relentless action now.
- **Calling** – I believe it is irrevocable regardless of who says "yes" or "no."

Remember, no matter where you are or what your struggle may be, you are in the right place. Whether this is your first attempt at doing something different or if this is your 25th. It's never too late to restart your vision. You are not too old. You are not too young. You know everyone you need to know. You have the resources that you need. Your market is not too saturated, because it is missing you. Anything you need, beyond what you already have, God will provide. Once you say "Yes, God I believe," and commit to the process, you will be one step closer to manifestation.

God has not forgotten about you. In fact, He knows your name and He desires to do "exceedingly and abundantly above all that you could ask or think!"(Ephesians 3:20). Whenever you feel like things are not working out like they should or you are not moving as fast as you desire, revisit these core components: Vision, Belief, Execution, and Calling. Let this chapter be the one you revisit and study. Contrary to Dorothy's famous line in *The Wizard of Oz*, "There's no place like home," there's no place I'd rather be than in God's will, versus my own.

Reflections and Learnings

COURAGEOUS STEP #4

How Can I Move Forward?

"Don't just watch, be present in the moment."

received a tweet that really resonated with me. It was from a woman who read an article I wrote on LinkedIn, about moving from your career to your calling. In the article, I mentioned how your calling continues to whisper to you until you say "yes." She said her calling was no longer whispering, *it was singing*! Can you relate to that feeling? That knock you hear on your heart does one of two things: 1) gets louder and faster the closer you move toward it, or 2) becomes this faint nagging sound that gets quieter the longer you wait to answer it.

Whether the knock on your heart can barely be heard or it feels like someone is about to break down a door, you are probably feeling one of these three things: (i) Continuously thinking about it all the time, yet sitting on the sideline; (ii) About to jump in with trepidation; or (iii) Getting ready to make your biggest move yet! All of these thoughts and emotions are normal, as long as you are continuously moving toward what God keeps whispering in your heart.

Let's take a look at a common pyramid thought process, and three women who identify with each one.

Starting from the bottom, Deborah is the Passive Thinker. She has never considered attending a meeting to interact others moving in her dream profession, let alone imagining a world outside of her stressful day-to-day. As a divorced, single mother of two adolescent girls, Deborah is driven to pay the bills and provide for the ongoing activities for the girls, including dance, theater, karate, and basketball. Deborah always sees the glass empty as there will never be enough time in her day to step outside her exhausting norm.

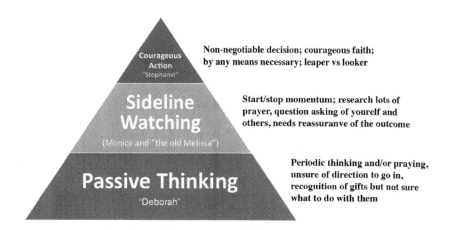

Courageous Action "Stephanie" — Non-negotiable decision; courageous faith; by any means necessary; leaper vs looker

Sideline Watching (Monica and "the old Melissa") — Start/stop momentum; research lots of prayer, question asking of yourelf and others, needs reassuranve of the outcome

Passive Thinking "Deborah" — Periodic thinking and/or praying, unsure of direction to go in, recognition of gifts but not sure what to do with them

With over 20 years as a real estate paralegal with mortgage credentials, she has longed to start a consulting business to help homeowners navigate through the maze and pitfalls of home buying. She is well aware of the recognized names and banking institutions offering similar services, but she believes she has a niche and a personal service that none of them have tapped into. Deborah started a business plan eight years ago to set up her business locally. To date, she has not given it another thought.

Like the old me, Monica has been a Sideline Watcher for over 10 years now. She has made great strides in continuing her education by obtaining a Masters in International Business. She has always been fascinated with various cultures and languages. Monica's dream was to create a global service-oriented assimilation company. She has personally traveled the world and engaged in lengthy conversations with several tour guides who fueled her passion for offices around the world. The more she travels, the more she is encouraged and sees how she can help those headed to the United States for work, business, vacation, or permanent residence.

Unfortunately, Monica became discouraged when hundreds of international online "Meet Ups" took off, which was her part of her long-term business plan. She felt deflated. All that was left for her to do was to continue in her job as a quality assurance manager for a large corporation. Yet, every now and then, she pulls out the business plan, tweaks a few pages and places it back in her desk drawer. Monica is still stuck in the middle.

The empty space between the realization where change was needed and the day that I actually began my journey (for real this time), was long. There were many times when I constantly worried about what was next, talked about what was next, and merely daydreamed about what was next. I was caught up in what I call "The Matrix," just thinking, planning, and praying in a non-productive, repetitive cycle. I was doing just enough to make myself feel like I was moving forward, when in actuality I was standing still.

Remember Stephanie? After being downsized, she left her corporate HR position and enrolled in a music therapy program to the dismay of her father. Stephanie took *Courageous Action* and is top of the pyramid, doing what it takes to walk out her dream. My ultimate wish is that we have a lot more Stephanie's as role models.

> *"Moving from the bottom up is the only*
> *way to go to the next level."*

Each move up the pyramid requires you to be willing to let go of some things and be willing to change where you are. I remember when I came across the first bathrobe I bought when I went to college 20 years ago. It was a long green robe that was the absolute BEST thing to have on the coldest winter day in the mountains. I loved putting it on any time I felt like I needed comfort and familiarity after a long tough day of classes. When I recently came across it, my gut reaction was, "Oh my gosh, I have to get rid of this thing!" But the thought of parting with something comfortable, had me second-guessing that decision. *Well, maybe I need to keep it a little longer. Technically, there's nothing wrong with it. I might need it someday,* I thought. Do any of these thoughts sound familiar? These are the same thoughts we process anytime we begin to think about transition and letting things go.

> *"The biggest antagonist to the pursuit of what it is in*
> *our heart is the fear of losing our own comfort!"*

Are you willing to leave from where you are to get started on where you are going? Most of the turmoil exist in our hearts because of our inability to make a non-negotiable decision to move forward by *any means necessary*. Instead, we think, ask our friends, pray about it, and then pray again. All the while, never fully making a conscious commitment and a stating a definitive, "YES" to the thing that God put in our spirit, which is the thing people are waiting on us to do. As long as there is not a definitive, "YES," there will always be an indefinite "MAYBE" where there is no action. The more options you give to yourself, the more ways you find to escape your commitment.

There are certain circumstances in our lives that require us to make a drastic leap to change. Like the time I moved from Virginia Beach, VA to Charlotte, NC to pursue a new career opportunity without knowing anyone. I had gone through a layoff at my former job and started applying for organizational development positions around the country. One day, I got a call from a recruiter in Salisbury, NC. I said, "Salis...who?" The recruiter told me they were located 40 miles north of Charlotte, a city I had visited once and loved. The only caveat was that I did not have a friend or a family member who lived in Charlotte. It was the biggest move of my life; to date, anyways.

All I knew was that there was something in front of me that was greater than what was behind me. The job description literally had my name written on it! It was a God moment, for sure. In less than six weeks, I interviewed, accepted the offer, and packed my bags to see exactly what amazing things were in store. Was it easy? No. Was it worth it? YES!

I am sure you can recount times and seasons in your life when you had to say goodbye to where you were in order to get to where you are now. Remember the sacrifices you took. The investments you made. It was a decision that you did not take lightly. The impact of leaving your family and close friends is a major shift but absolutely necessary in most instances.

Self-Reinvention Faith

When transitioning to something greater, our limited mindset tends to focus on what we will lose, instead of focusing on all that we will gain. The fear of not making as much money that you are currently making or whether there will be an opportunity to supplement your income creeps into your mind. Once you realize in your heart that you actually have everything to gain, you should move full speed ahead.

Unfortunately, most of us have been programmed to dream from a corporate perspective. That is to earn six-figures, double-digit bonuses, and climb the corporate ladder as high as you can go until retirement. I am not going to sugar coat, this can be a GREAT life for many. There's no doubt that for aspiring entrepreneurs, a high salary, corporate perks, and esteem are hard to walk away from. However, once you truly grab hold of the power and awesomeness of the God that you serve, you should be even more determined to make the transition. Just imagine the possibilities of God's blessing if He already blessed you with one level of success. How much more do you think He can replenish it? Will there be some hard times? More than likely!

As your faith kicks in, something amazing happens. God shows you that this walk is not based on what *you* can do or how you can provide for your family. It's based upon how He can provide for you *every* day. One of the things my best friend said to me repeatedly in the beginning of my leap was, "Melissa this is not about your mortgage being paid, this is about your calling." Her tone was always with an assurance to let me know that bills were the least of my worries because He had already done what He promised.

To be honest, the person who had the courage to start the business but their current potential is far below where they should be, is worse off than the person who never took the chance. Once you've taken the leap, it must be bold and fearless. You must look for ways to enter new markets or offer new product lines. Picture this, "What if you made your leap and opened yourself to the opportunity to truly experience more of God's amazing gifts, in addition to where you are now?

A Bright Horizon

One of my biggest fears is getting to the end of my life and seeing what God had for me that I was too afraid to try. Similar to how I am sure others like Oprah Winfrey, Serena Williams, and the late Steve Jobs would have felt if they never took the risks they did in the beginning. Each one of them were up against great odds, and pressure to succeed. Fortunately, their desire and determination to succeed outweighed every naysayers criticizing words.

COURAGEOUS SPOTLIGHT

THE SKY IS <u>NOT</u> THE LIMIT

Meet Courageous Dr. Jedidah Isler
Astrophysicist, Speaker, Advocate for women of
color in STEM and Academic Entrepreneur.

M: You're an astrophysicist and one of the most down to earth scientists I know. Tell everyone how you came across one of the most compelling and unique careers.

J: My story for how I got into it is pretty simple. I was about 12 years old and I had the privilege of living in a place where you could see the night sky. That was critical for me because I would go outside, lay in the grass, and look at the night sky for hours. It was so beautiful. I found it soothing, calming, and aesthetically pleasing. It wasn't until I got to about 12 that it became known to me that one could study the sky as a job and could have a career understanding the night sky. As soon as I heard that, I said, "this is what we're going to do with our life, Jedidah."

M: While it's easy to say you did it one class at a time, there's something that happens at each juncture point where there are roadblocks, speed bumps, and obstacles. It's the courage to persevere. Talk about what that looked like for you in your journey.

J: One of the key elements when I talk to people that I try to convey is this notion that everything looks beautifully rendered when you're looking in hindsight. You read someone's bio and they did this and that. It's very clear, concise, and ordered. It makes sense. But that is not the lived experience of the actual journey. Actually it's like, "Should I do THIS or should I do THAT? Oh, well, THAT didn't work out, so I'm not doing it."

I've been enamored lately with all these truisms you hear as you go through life. "The journey of a thousand miles begins with one step." And I always thought that those things were super corny. Seriously, who says that? But honestly, what happened was I realized that it actually is that. It is the case that deciding to take one more science course over another possible course, or deciding to study an hour or two longer, instead of going to parties – those things add up. They accumulate into a bigger movement than any particular step itself belies. It's the courage, or maybe the obnoxiousness to continue to take the first step, the next step after that, and to take a step that you don't know where it's going. All of that is a part of, what it looks like now, a global courage to keep going.

M: I need you to talk about when it looks like you don't know where you're going.

J: The idea is that it's pushing back against this notion that all is known when you begin. Or you know where you're going to end up when you start. And the truth of the matter is if you're doing it right, you have no idea. If you are doing courage right, if you are doing exploration right, if you are doing investigation properly, then you don't actually know the answer when you start. You may know the general direction you want to go. I've always known I wanted to go toward astrophysics, but I didn't know at 12 I wanted to study black holes, do observational astronomy, or travel around the world. I didn't know all those things came with it. What's critical is the step from the known to the unknown, which takes quite a bit of courage.

M: Isn't that like science? Being able to explore what you do know, then go out to explore what's unknown and how it even came about. We've talked about the courage to persevere, to persist, and the willingness to go from the known into the unknown, which you did. That led you to an historical moment of becoming the first African American woman to graduate from Yale with a Ph.D. in Astrophysics.

J: I remember that. I guess one thing you mentioned that was worth pointing out was when I got there, I said, "Where are the black people?" Where do they sit?" I was trying to understand that and myself in context of a very white space. I had gone to a historically black college and university for my bachelor's and first master's. I was very used to seeing highly educated black people and brown people around. So to get to a place where there wasn't that, it was very daunting.

People often ask me, "How did you feel being the first black woman to walk across that stage?" I say, "Well, really I walked across that stage as Dr. Jedidah Isler," and that was the visceral feeling overall. I walked across the stage to, you and my other family members screaming out for what we had as a team, as a unit, endured.

M: The thing I love about your story is that it doesn't stop there. After walking across the stage, you could easily go and do your work. You could go and be a scientist. But there's something about you that says there's more. I look at it as going from existing in a career to transforming an industry. I think about your advocacy for women of color in STEM and your monthly Vanguard video series, for like-minded women of color in STEM. Talk to us about becoming a truth-teller and what is your message?

J: I appreciate that. One of the core tenets of the kind of work that I do, is that there is no way to separate my identity from the work. I'm not an astrophysicist and that's it. I exist as a black woman, as a woman of color, as a millennial, as all of these things. All of these things exist simultaneously, with me having picked up the credentials to be an astrophysicist. When we talk about truth-telling, I felt like that's what I had to do. Me negotiating the space of astronomy, physics, and astrophysics, as it were, and negotiating Ivy League institutions, required something of me personally as much as it did intellectually. When I finished, there was a lot I learned. I gained so much strength from the experience. I got some pretty legit knocks, scrapes, and bumps. But I also learned to be confident in my own ability in my voice, even if that voice was different than the voices around me.

There's an interesting statistic I learned later. It's that black women, in particular, are more likely than black men to be in these upper level fields and institutions for a number of sociological reasons. One of the outcomes is that black women are often not feeling included in this space, so they get swept up into this buzzword of "diversity", but they're not actually being included. The spaces they are being brought into are not inclusive, so they end up feeling very lonely. They tend to feel lonelier than any other demographic group. Having a place for them to come together and identify as both black women and STEM-icists, as I like to call them, STEM practitioners, no matter what the field. It gives room for them to be fully who they are in their black woman-ness, in their latina-ness, or their first nation woman-ness – whatever it is, and also be a highly skilled, technical expert.

M: To be able to exist in those multiple places and find yourself and your voice is intriguing to the soul to say, "I'm different, but I know I belong here." One of the things you call yourself is an academic entrepreneur. One of the most powerful quotes I heard you say is, "If you say "no" to me, I view that as a lack of vision on your part." Talk about how you were able to arrive at that mindset in your journey and your career?

J: I appreciate you saying that, because it truly was a journey. I did not wake up and know that one day. That came as the culmination of many experiences and the culmination of many self-assessments and reflection. When I'm mentoring young women who are coming up in the field or in STEM in general, I often say that, "difference does not mean bad." Just because something is different, doesn't make it less than. That is critical in finding a place to exist in the world. That "Yes, I am different!" I actually enjoy being different. I like being different by being a black woman. But what I'm unwilling to accept is that because I'm different, I am less than. That took a lot of time, especially in the academic space. In fact, I honor, respect, and appreciate my difference. That's a critical component right there.

The second thing, going to that quote – it's funny, because literally what somebody asked was, "Well, what do you do when somebody says no to you?" And I said, "I view no as a suggestion. I appreciate that no. That's a really great suggestion. I'm going to try yes on for size. You know, just try it out and see how it feels." We ask too many questions. We ask permission too often. That's first. Second, often you're asking people who have no more authority over what you're trying to do than you do. It literally is an opinion. "Can I do this?" How do they know? How do they know what you can do? They have no clue. No one knows until you do it. When I said that, what I really was saying was I have a vision in my mind for the way see my future, for the way I want my career to go, and for the impact I want to have. So when I ask you for some component of that and you tell me no, you have no idea what I'm envisioning. I arrived at that by a bunch of little, small experiments where I allowed myself to think, "Well, I know that this person just said no, but what if I try something over here? Would that work?" And lo and behold, it would work. Let's be clear, sometimes it didn't. Everything I try does not always work. But sometimes it did and in critical moments, it did. "Well, if that works, why am I even asking permission for something that is completely up for whoever wants to do the work?" and it evolves over time, when I recognize I have quite a bit of agency in how my life turns out.

You mention this notion of entrepreneurship and how I view myself as being an academic entrepreneur. I enjoy the academic portion of what I do. But I feel like there's a lot of room to self-direct, self-create, to explore, even in the sector of academia. Those two things come together for me: the notion of being an academic entrepreneur and having a vision, and not necessarily allowing anybody to arbitrarily tell me what I can and cannot do.

M: That space in itself is an evolution, to be able to realize that when people say no to us, it's a lack of vision on their part. Tell us about what you have coming up next?

J: One of the things I am most excited about right now is the Vanguard: STEM series. There's a hashtag: #VanguardSTEM. What that stands for is Vanguard: Conversations with Women of Color in STEM. It's a monthly Google Hangout. I'm the host and I bring on women of color who are in STEM in some capacity. They have a STEM degree, they're working in STEM, or they might have moved out of STEM and into some other field. It explores the richness and robustness of this lived experience of the larger group of women of color in STEM. They offer strategic advice, but at the same time as well as show a representation of who does STEM. And I'm still doing research on blazars and trying to understand how they work.

Jedidah has literally reached for the stars, grabbed them, and is implementing ways for others to snatch even bigger ones. While gender and race may appear to be an obstacle in your vision, don't give up. Work harder and learn more. Watch the status quo and atmosphere shift to make room for you!

WALKING OUT STEP #4

Like Jedidiah and other successful courageous movers, I had to take risks to ensure that my most passionate desires and biggest calling to date, was answered in the affirmative.

I know I am here...

...to inspire, spark change, and stand in the gap for women to get out of the box and pursue a new beginning that allows them to build the life, career, and business they want.

I know I am here...

...to help leaders just like you move from your career to your calling.

I know you are here...

... to _____

Once you really know, you have to be willing to move forward. You have to be willing to let go of what is familiar. Moving from your career to your calling will require you to say "yes," again and again! It's not ironic that mega television writer, creator and producer, Shonda Rhimes penned her bestseller, *Year of Yes: How to Dance It Out, Stand in the Sun, and Be Your Own Person.* Everyone has certain hang ups or insecurities, even when they have achieved a level of success others dream of. In the book, Shonda sheds her introvert self, and takes on everything she feared or made her uncomfortable.

Similarly, your leap will require you to get uncomfortable beyond your own definition of discomfort. The best and biggest way to achieve your dreams is consistent movement. Sometimes the movement will feel like small steps and you will wonder if you are moving at all. Other times, it will feel like huge leaps beyond what your legs can stretch, that reposition you overnight. Your focus should not be on breaking the Olympic long jump record, but on making a large leap to qualify.

PART II

DECLARE YOUR DECISION
(THE WHEN)

COURAGEOUS STEP #5

CAN YOU SWIM?

"The only thing missing from your future is you!

Afraid of Deep Water

Most people talk about their goals and dreams in an aspirational sense. It usually starts with the same opener, "One day, I will..." I have heard the dreams of friends, family, and colleagues moving into to new roles, starting their own businesses, changing careers, starting a non-profit, and going back to school. I absolutely LOVE hearing it all! What I dislike about hearing their dreams are the answers to my questions:

"What are you doing about it?
"Have you started working on it?"

I've received so many "nothing" and "no" responses that I get a bit annoyed. If you truly have a dream, these are valid questions. Ever since we were children we asked questions. We wanted to know the answer to everything. As adults we are wired to want to know how it is all going to turn out before we begin. That level of clarity provides an assurance and safety net. It also does not require faith. It means that you are relying on yourself and your own understanding. Dr. Martin Luther King Jr. once said, "Faith is taking the first step, even when you don't see the whole staircase." Most of the time you will not know, but you just have to start walking. By trying to figure out the end, before we even say "yes" to the beginning, we forgo or delay the pursuit of the very thing God has in store for us.

Still Sitting on the Sideline

What happens when we say "yes" in our hearts, but not with our hands and feet? Sometimes we end up sitting on the edge of something, watching things happen around us. All my life I have absolutely LOVED water, water sports, and lots of lazy days on the beach. However, up until my mid-30s, I didn't know how to swim. I was terrified of deep water and the possibility of drowning. I tried swimming lessons several times throughout the course of my life, but for one reason or another, it never worked out. Then finally one day, there I was with a swim coach sitting on the edge of the deep pool – sitting on the sideline once again. He gave me step-by-step instructions several times over the following 30 minutes, but it did not matter. I was too afraid. After stalling for over 30 minutes, praying to the sun, the heavens, the moon, and the stars, I was finally able to lower myself into seven feet of water. I spent a few minutes getting acclimated to the water, started splashing around and finally screamed out, "Hey, it's not that bad in here!" How often is the fear we have greater than the outcome of the experience?

What are you sitting on the edge of? What I've found is that so many of us sit on the edge of life, the same way I sat on the edge of that pool. We sit there, hedging back and forth, looking at what we want to do. Yet we remain, paralyzed about our future. The truth is that most of us end up waiting on the wrong thing. We sit on the sidelines for so long because we are waiting on this overwhelming sense of peace, calmness, and level of confidence that IT WILL work out before we make any major moves.

This predicament reminds me of the story in John 5:1-15 of the man sitting by the Pool of Bethesda for 38 years waiting for his healing in the water. He was literally waiting for someone to lift him up and bring him to the water when he could have made it there on his own! If you are waiting for a miracle, know that the miracle happens when you take the step on your own initiative.

Instead of saying, "Yes, God I'll go," and trusting in the process, what we really mean is "Yes, God I'll go as long as I know everything is going to be okay!" The presence of any doubt emotions does not mean it is a given fact that you are supposed to start or stop. In fact, many times they are simply the emotions that come along with change. Anytime you do something that is beyond you, it sends you into an unfamiliar territory. You will always have some level of heightened emotions because swimming in deep water for the first time is new and unknown. It does not mean you should not be doing it. Rather do it to finally get it out of your system.

The Misconceptions of Saying "Yes!"

I should move forward with my goals and dreams ONLY if:	I should NOT move forward with my goals and dreams if:
<ul><li>I feel calm</li><li>I feel peace</li><li>I feel assurance</li><li>I can predict the outcome</li></ul>	<ul><li>I feel any level of fear</li><li>Wonder if it will work</li><li>Have anxiety</li><li>Have doubts</li><li>Worry</li></ul>

We wait on this false sense of security we think is supposed to exist every time we stand on the edge of the deep end of the pool. If we wait to pursue new things because we expect to feel 110% confident, nothing will happen. That situation honestly does not exist. If someone claims they are confident, I have to wonder if that person is really stretching his or her boundaries.

I get it. No one likes to feel out of control. However, that is where God operates. He is not in a box trying to do what has already been done. There are people, industries, and even countries that need the innovative and creative ideas He has given to you and only you. Even when you feel like you don't measure up, truthfully, you don't have to, He's put things in motion to set you up with people and contracts to give you the confidence to move in your new role. Rest easy, the path has already been made straight on your behalf.

COURAGEOUS SPOTLIGHT

DESTINED FOR DESIGN

Meet Courageous Nikki Klugh
CEO and Principal Designer of The Nikki Klugh Design Group

M: I want to know about the Nikki Klugh before she started this amazing company. What were you doing before you started Nikki Klugh Design Group?
N: Right out of high school, I was encouraged to major in engineering. There was a big push to recruit women in engineering, as there still is. I was a sharp student in math and science and it seemed like it would be a good fit. In college, I majored in chemical engineering, but I did not find it exciting. I was engaged, so after I got married and started having kids, I called it quits. I was home raising my babies. We have four amazing young men now and in that process, I did home party plans. I sold Pampered Chef, BeautiControl makeup, and other things to get me out and talking to other women. That

sparked the entrepreneurial spirit in me, with the idea of having my own business, setting my own hours, and working around the needs of my family. I did it for about six years.

When my youngest son was born, we moved yet again, and I was faced with building a new team in a new city and I felt like, "If I'm going to do all this work, it should be something for myself." I was still selling, still doing some of the things it would take to start a company on my own. It was around the emergence of HGTV, seeing designers on TV, and saying, "Wow! This is what I've always really wanted to do!" I'd go far back as I can remember, being 8 years old, rearranging my room, painting, and doing decorating projects with my mom. But, I didn't think you could make any money in this career. I associated design with art and artists, and didn't want to be a starving artist myself. I thought, "I'll do engineering and make lots of money." Obviously, that didn't hold my interest. It came full circle and I went back to school, got a degree in interior design, and worked for another designer for a couple of years. Then I got my first big client. I felt prepared and ready to step out on my own, and I did that for many years in Palo Alto, CA.

M: An amazing transition story. Here's the thing I love about it the best: You said, "If I'm going to have to do all of this, I might as well be doing it for myself."

N: It's so true! We work hard day in and day out, whether we are making our own dreams come true or helping someone else build their dreams. It's all hard work. Anything worthwhile is going to be hard work.

M: In reference to rebuilding your own team and doing it for you, that's a pretty big job. You started building a business that's not just you, but having a team with junior designers, principal designers, and more. One where you're able to, not only serve clients in San Diego, but all over the country. Tell us about that transition. How did you say, "Nikki, you can do this," and find the courage and faith to do it?

N: Well, quite frankly, it didn't happen all at once. It was baby steps. I say that because when I branched out on my own, it was with the intention of working part-time around my family, controlling my schedule. Now that I look back, it was a well-paid hobby because I didn't have systems, I didn't have a team, and I was doing everything on my own. I was making good money, but I wasn't really running a company or a well-oiled business. That didn't really happen until 2008, and as everyone knows, it is one of those magical dates that brings back all types of memories, good or bad. That's when the Recession hit and everything started falling apart. In my profession, pretty much everything dried up. I was here in San Diego, in a brand new town, looking around and I'm my own best client. I had no clients, I was decorating my own home and thinking, "Oh my gosh, what am I going to do?"

At that point, all I knew to do was to go back to being a stay-at-home mom. That's honorable, I'm serving my family, I won't be spinning my wheels, but the thought of that broke my heart. The thought of never designing again or serving people in this manner was sad to me. I found and got connected to a very powerful group of people – other entrepreneurs that had courage and the fire to do whatever was necessary. My vision became enlarged. I could see what was possible and the things I needed to get in place in order to grow my company step by step. I was able to gain more understanding on what a business really is.

M: One of the things you mentioned was realizing it happened in baby steps. That is the best and only way to build a company. What would you tell a woman who is on the brink of what's next for her? Similar to you, when they think about if they never did it again, they would be heartbroken?

N: One of things is that your passion, something that drives you, excites you, and has you jumping out of bed in the morning, is given to you. It's a God-given gift, a God-given desire and we may not all be called to serve in that manner to earn an income. Not everything is going to produce an income. But I bet that if you explore further, take a bigger view of what is driving you, you can find a way to work in that somehow. Don't let it die, whether it becomes your new business or in support of someone else. That desire and passion has to be fulfilled or you're just withering on the vine. Dig deep and take some time with it. It doesn't have to be an overnight decision. It doesn't have to be this lifelong commitment, just take one step toward it.

I actually would go back and mention, to find a community that supports you. Find and associate with people who can see beyond what you see. We only have one perspective of ourselves. But if we are seen through the eyes of others, and allow them to speak to us – even in the voice of God, how He sees us and wants us to operate – that's crucial in breaking past your own limiting foresight. Being in that community of people saying "You should have your own TV show," helped me to see now I can. It's getting closer, expanding five years down the road; we could have our own product, textiles, and furniture. That is an exciting thought. It's a whole new business!

One of the key pieces to this puzzle of courageous steps is recognizing that all of the steps fit cohesively together. Some steps may seem repetitious, but in order to truly learn and grow, repetition is necessary. I applaud Nikki's actions when her market dried up in 2008. Instead of taking down her designer shingle, she mustered the courage to connect with other entrepreneurs to help brainstorm and plan to grow her business. What will you do when your well runs dry? Stroll down the road, borrow and glean from your neighbor's well.

WALKING OUT STEP #5

Drowning is not an option

I received an email from a young woman one day that ended with the word:

"Help!"

She wrote, "*Thank you for your emails. Last Sunday's sermon really spoke to me. I realize things are no coincidences. The pastor talked about taking a step first. About an hour or so later after service, I received your email "Do you dread going to work on Monday."* I just smiled.

"*Today at work, everyone received a 1.2% raise. We have a new boss because the last boss was recently fired. Melissa, I calculated this raise to be $12 extra a week. Here are two comments that I received: One of my co-workers - "At least it is more than you were getting before." One of my managers- "Every bit counts." Everyone around me seems so satisfied with their jobs. Wow Melissa, I couldn't believe it. I am grateful that the new boss was thoughtful enough to give everyone a raise, and I am grateful that I have a job, but wow $12.00. It doesn't even fill my car up with gas! Melissa, am I being ungrateful? I thank God every day for all of His* *blessings... income included. However, I am so frustrated with this job. I am willing to jump off this Ferris wheel and into my dreams. Help!"*

Her level of frustration was high because her level of thinking was beyond the small-mindedness of those around her. Of course she was grateful for the 1.2% raise. But she knew God had given her so many gifts and talents that were worth so much more. Like many, she sat uncomfortably where she was, yet was too afraid to swim in the unknown deep water.

"Don't look for permanent comfort in a temporary place."

I easily related to her email because when I was in Corporate America, I felt trapped in a life that seemed too good to leave, but was unfulfilling. I simply didn't value myself enough to make the big leap. There was always the great raise that was never quite enough to make me feel like I was making a difference in people's lives. There was also a promotion that seemed to appease, rather than empower me to lead. I was tired of being frustrated with this "just enough" experience. It wasn't until I had a conversation with a mentor who had shared with me that I would always feel frustrated as long as my vision was bigger than where I was. She said, "You're looking for permanent comfort in a temporary place!" That epiphany allowed me to realize I was wrestling with trying to stay somewhere I was never intended to stay. I could no longer sit on edge of something great, I had to *become* something great.

Although the woman who sent me the email received a meager raise as a motivator, she still feared she would be making the wrong decision if she quit. She was in search of the peace and feeling of calm that I spoke of earlier. She wanted to know if she stepped out, started investing in herself and her dreams, would it be okay? She found herself sitting on the edge of her greatness, but was still afraid to jump. Of course, for most people, hastily quitting their job would not be a wise move. However, you have to get to the point where you are willing to do what it takes to make your vision a reality and then jump in, and get wet all by yourself!

COURAGEOUS STEP #6

IS THIS THE RIGHT TIME?

"Taking a courageous first step does not mean you're quitting your job today!

Flashback to a season of restlessness years ago. I thought I was ready for my dream. I had this bright idea that it was time to start. There was this burning desire that I was supposed to be doing something more than corporate HR. I daydreamed about it in meetings. I constantly thought about it throughout the day and I definitely could not go any length of time without talking about it with close friends. I was ready! It was time! So much so that my heart physically ached for it.

Sunday evenings became *the worst*! The bittersweet end to my temporary weekend escape from a life and career I had outgrown. After all, I was *not* supposed to be in that career forever anyway. The benefits of all my hard work were rewarding. After awhile, I started to go into each week dreading the monotony, lack of inspiration, and lack of purposeful impact that I knew I could make elsewhere; beyond the four walls of that brick office building.

So I did what any passionate person like myself would do. I marched into work with a strong conviction and turned in my two weeks' notice. I was off to change the world in just two weeks! I was READY! After all, I had been thinking about this since the 12th grade! I'm fully-grown now. The only problem was that I did not have a plan. At least, not a concrete one, anyway. This realization caused me to pause and reflect if this was the right move after all. It wasn't. So, I humbly went to my boss during that two week time frame and said never mind!

*"The right decisions at the wrong time
are still the wrong decisions."*

Most people wait until their career transition is forced or either they can't take it anymore. Both of those options are too late. No one wants to go to their boss like I did, and ask to have their job back. It was an awkward experience to say the least. I made a big mistake when I quit. I took the leap without a parachute. Of course, I knew I was jumping without a job. However, I also jumped **without a plan**. All I had was the tremendous desire and compelling feeling to go, and go NOW!

After picking up my pride and having the "I made a mistake" conversation with my boss, I kept working. Luckily for me, I loved my job and just had to figure out what to do with the growing anticipation in my heart. So, I decided to create a more strategic transition towards my entrepreneurial goals. However, believe it or not, after making the huge mistake of quitting without thinking through the long-term impact, I made another huge mistake that cost me both time and money.

Now that I was ready to be more strategic about the things I knew God was calling me to do, I started working diligently after work and on the weekends. Then, as I am sure you have experienced in your own pursuits, work got busy, life got busier, and my plans became less and less of a priority. Over the next several *years* I would go through many seasons of starts and stops.

I could not understand how I was so easily derailed and lost focus so quickly if this was supposed to be so important to me. It would still be a while before I figured out what would change the entire game for me when I finally launched to where I am now, a couple of years later.

1. **Lack of commitment leads to lack of progress**
2. **Non-negotiable plans lead to radical success!**

I know many of you may be completely over the jobs that you have. You may be ready to take the leap or you may be ready to be successful at the leap you have already taken. Your success will come when you make a decision to fully commit to the dream that God has placed inside of you. When that happens, the journey becomes non-negotiable, whether you have a full-time job, a family, or other big commitments. Whether it is easy or whether it is hard, you will be ready once you have fully committed. Are you 100% committed? Have you made the thing that God has called you to do non-negotiable or is it still up for grabs?

> *"The best plans are those that are made while you have the time to make them."*

After reading a passage from Pastor Steven Furtick's, *Sun Stand Still*, on audacious faith, my heart literally jumped. He said that all he had was, "Just a burning conviction that there has to be more to life than a 401(k), additional square footage, soccer leagues, and church as usual." His book conveyed exactly what was in my heart, that my existence was far too great to simply live out a mundane, routine life. A life where it always looked like I excelled to the outside world, but one where I was stopping just short of the purpose I knew could change the world.

I felt for the first time that someone truly understood me and expressed the ache in my heart exactly as I felt it. Reading it felt like a weight had been lifted. I often felt guilty for even wrestling with the thought of walking away from it all. However, my heart's continuous cry was, "God, there has to be more!" I still say it today, but it feels much better saying it while moving toward where I'm going, versus saying it in the stagnation from where I was. I had to learn that I was not walking away from something, but I was walking *toward* something greater.

While my initial thoughts of escaping the corporate rat race were crazy, I began to realize that there were countless people just like me, all stuck between places where they exist in comfort, rather than thriving in their purpose. One of my corporate clients once asked, "Doesn't everyone hate their job?" My heart broke at the very thought of her question. Although I don't believe it is true, I do believe that many are stuck, or just too comfortable to leave the place that they've known forever.

Ready, Set Go!

I was willing to put everything I worked for on the line. At the beginning of 2013, I knew it was the right time. I had come to my breaking point. My goals extended far beyond my corporate role. I became too uncomfortable in my own comfort zone and I was tired of sitting on the sideline ready to start my vision. That was the year I decided it did not matter what my work schedule looked like, because I was getting ready to adventure into the uncertainty of entrepreneurship. I was ready to go after what had been chasing after me my whole life, my purpose.

I spent the first half of the year planning and promoting my first event while I worked full-time. By that summer, I made the definitive decision it was time to transition. I just needed to figure out the "right time." I was so overwhelmed with excitement and momentum, I didn't know whether to turn in my two weeks' notice immediately, wait until the following spring when bonuses would be distributed, or wait another full year?

Our organization had already gone through significant changes for several years prior to 2013, but that year was unprecedented. It was the biggest shake up (or should I say shake down) in the previous 50 years of the company. Leading up to our department restructure, my boss continuously reassured me the changes were not about headcount. Our organization had already gone through so much earlier in the year, she wanted me to eliminate any additional anxiety of my team. They were on pins and needles after having watched countless leaders and associates walk out of the door months before.

As things began to finalize, my boss set up a meeting with me and shared our new org structure. The bad news was my role was simultaneously being eliminated and combined into a national role, instead of local. The good news was that I was presented several other opportunities that had great leadership potential. All I could think about was, "Oh, man! If I take one of these roles, this is going to throw a wrench into my plans! I was trying to leave!" No way could I accept a new leadership role and say, "Excuse me, but I decided I am actually leaving in a couple a week's!" Taking on a new role would easily mean another 12-18 months with the organization. A step I was not sure I wanted to take.

I went home that weekend and ranked the positions in my head based on my passions. What would best position me for success in living out my long-term goals? Then I shared my thoughts with my boss and looked forward to our next conversation. I walked into her office to discuss next steps, wondering if our conversation would result in a promotion or a lateral move in our new structure. What happened next, was neither. Instead, I heard, "Melissa, this is hard for me to say, but after some consideration, there is no place for you on the leadership team!"

Sound the alarm! What did you just say? Repeat that? Did she just give me the answer to the on-going debate about when I was supposed to transition? For most people, this would be one of the most devastating conversations they heard in their career. For me, it was one of the *most divine*! I knew that conversation was truly a God moment.

All the times I thought about the exact moment I would transition from my career to my calling was finally over. I had my answer. I was beyond excited and could not wait for her to finish her spiel, because I had work to do. Not only that, but I was getting on a plane the next day to become certified with the John Maxwell Team, the #1 leadership expert team in the world! Talk about God's timing! I could not have planned it better myself!

My life changed because that was the day I made a **non-negotiable decision** to pursue my dreams, once and for all. Yes I had a nudge, but it was the day I finally went from just thinking to doing. I went from sitting on the sideline to doing all the things I wanted to do. I began to see momentum, support, and creativity like never before. I knew it was one of the biggest moments of my life.

Not only did I know, the world knew too, at least my little world. Filled with a mix of emotions from the news, I called my best friend immediately. I heard a piercing scream of excitement when I told her the news. Not only did I know what that day meant for my future, she knew, too. So did my mom, and the next friend, and all those I had shared my dreams with through the years.

We often have people around us that are cheering for us and waiting on us to tap into the space we are destined to be in. Every time someone cheered with an excitement greater than my own, I wanted to say, "Didn't you just hear that I got laid off?" However, it didn't matter. We all knew that the layoff was divinely orchestrated to launch me into the very thing I was born to do; inspire, coach, and train others.

What's stopping you from showing up to live out your gifts? I teach about taking the first step in my workshops. I encourage participants and help them identify the opportunities, resources, and people waiting to support them, that they will never be able to experience until they start. Our faith requires us to **believe** that whatever we need will be there when we need it.

Taking the first step does not mean, "I am going to quit my job today." Nor does it mean that you will know when to transition from your job, or the exact start date of your new venture. All of the pieces to this courageous puzzle will not be at your fingertips. Being ready to take your first step simply means that you have finally made a ***non-negotiable decision*** that is a resounding, YES. After that, it's up to you to do your part and trust God to do the rest.

What does your part look like? It's quite simple and less overwhelming than you think. Just start with critical steps like:

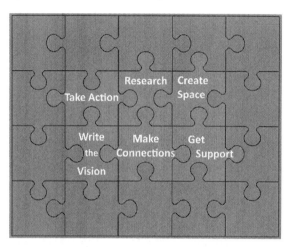

- **Research** – If there is one thing you can start doing, it is research. Research the role you want, the industry you want to move into, start-up costs, the skills required, the education or certification required, the cost to do it, similar business strategies, competition, and other key aspects. What would it take to bring your vision to life today?
- **Make connections** – Relationships are everything! Start building them now. Start thinking about the people who are doing what you already want to do. Create a list and begin to reach out to them. Most people are honored that you think of them so highly. I have an inner circle of friends and business colleagues that understand the magnitude of my goals and what it takes to achieve them. Who's on your team will be discussed in Courageous Step #8.
- **Create space** – Get rid of the excuses popping into your head. There will never be enough time in the day. You can make time for what you really want to do. Start with an hour every few days to focus on key tasks you need to accomplish. Will it take some sacrifice? Of course!

It may mean that you hang out less, go to bed earlier, or turn off your favorite TV shows.

- **Write the vision** – The vision in your head is one thing, the vision on paper is another. Be sure to write, rewrite, add, and edit the ideas that God gives you. Whether you think they can happen in six months or six years, having an active, visible, and organized vision plan maintains the momentum and motivation you need.

- **Take action** – Remember the only way to transition from your career to your calling is with movement. Think of what you can start doing now that enable you to learn, connect, or reflect. You can attend a networking event, write a blog, record a song, or whatever that first step looks like for you.

- **Get support** – You don't have to know all the answers. That is what people who have gone before you are for – to act as mentors and coaches and be your guide. They can easily answer the questions that keep you up at night.

Don't get so overwhelmed by the big picture. Focus on all the smaller pictures that create your complete vision. You can only put together one piece of a 500-piece puzzles at a time. As long as you keep a steady momentum, you will be moving towards your goal. Time waits for no one. It will continue to pass by regardless of your action or inaction.

WALKING OUT STEP #6

Now that you have moved past the excuses, the key is to keep going. Think about what has prevented you from making a non-negotiable decision towards the pressing dream in your heart. I am sure you are able to list several questions or obstacles that require serious thought. I do not want to minimize those needs and concerns. However, I would like you to begin to think about what it would look like if you started making consistent tangible steps toward your goals.

A Date with Destiny

Have you set a start date? A transition date? A Completion date? A date to contact someone? Setting dates for specific purposes creates sense of accountability, completion, and movement. Whatever you need to do, set a date to get it done. There's no time like the present! I recall when I set a date for my first event, I didn't want to tell anyone, not even my best friend. I knew telling someone, especially someone like her, would make it a reality, which meant that I would have to follow through. However, setting and sticking to dates for small things allow you to be able to accomplish some of the insurmountable things!

"The best results are the ones filled with action not contemplation!"

The transition from thinking about your goals to making a non-negotiable decision to pursue them with your whole heart is not trivial. But it's also not a continuous mountain top experience either. Your "yes" decision will be followed by lots of mundane moments. Your big moments are the summation of routine tasks you do consistently. For me, there are plenty of breakthrough times when I am traveling across the US speaking to audiences, and just as many when I am at home writing in my PJs. In order to create those peak experiences, God is waiting on your trust, commitment, and relentless pursuit of the small ones; especially when no one else is watching.

Whether you have a small inkling you are ready for change or you have an overwhelming sense of urgency that now is the time to move forward, start planning today. Get ready to take the leap, but make sure you create the plan you need first. The important thing to remember is that you consistently plan as you go. Do not wait until a crisis, like I did, or when you just can't take it anymore. Leaving a lucrative a career is just like having a baby; there is *never* going to be the exact right time to do it. You will always find something that gets in the way. Yet with the right plan, listening to God's voice, and faith in His word, you can make the decision as to the right time for your entrepreneurial transition. Do it while you have the time and security of your current income.

You are now free to roam in this journey, my friend!

PART III

DEVELOP YOUR PLAN
(THE HOW)

COURAGEOUS STEP #7

Did You Count the Costs?

"Money is only a tool to move your vision forward.
Don't let it hammer away your rational thinking."

oney, money, money! I have yet to meet a person starting a new venture say, "You know Melissa, I have so much money for my business, I just don't know what to do with it!" Actually, if someone said this to me, I would ask them to make a donation to the Courageous Life Academy! Scripture tells us that the love of money is the root of all evil (1 Timothy 6:10). However, it also advises us of its necessity to live and to use it both wisely and fairly. Point blank, you need *some* amount of money to make your leap.

For most of us, money is on our minds all the time. It is the lack of this tangible commodity that makes us constantly worry. We stress over how we can pay our bills and provide the basic necessities for our families. One of the major downfalls of most small businesses is the lack of start-up capital or sufficient capital to keep the business running longer than a few years. New business owners tend to underestimate the costs of operating expenses or have unrealistic revenue expectations. Many think, "This is such a great idea (or product), why wouldn't *everyone* want to buy it?"

"Suppose one of you wants to build a
tower. Won't you first sit down
and estimate the cost to see if you have
enough money to complete it?"
-LUKE 14:28

A common problem attributing to the unreal funding needs is that entrepreneurs actually base their target market on broad terms like "All consumers." Although millions of people could benefit from eating healthy food, it does not mean that millions are going to buy organic. Just think about it, there is enough medical evidence to tell us that processed meats, packaged food, and soda is bad for us. Yet it appears that 90% of supermarkets consist of aisles upon aisles of canned, bottled and packaged food. Eating healthy is great. Yet buying organic may be expensive for most. So even though fresh foods are better for us, Kraft Macaroni & Cheese, Pepsi and Entenmann's are not going out of business - at least not anytime soon. It is imperative that you diligently research, talk to others operating in your niche, and work with a business plan specialist to help you come up with realistic capital assumptions.

One Dollar and a Dream

Winning the lottery should not be factored into your start-up costs! Yes, it only costs one dollar, but the millions to one odds make your chances slim in time for making your leap. If you keep waiting for that *big* payday, you will ultimately miss out on your *big* purpose. There is really no magic money solution, nor does it grow on trees or fall from the sky. Obtaining extra money outside of your current job, takes hard work, creativity, and persistence. Of course there are some businesses that will not require a large start-up expense, such as selling services online.

However, regardless of your business model, if you are going to take a leap to operate in this new environment, it is wise to have enough savings to pay your bills and maintain a reasonable standard of living for at least six months to a year. That's because many businesses take a year or two to make a profit. If you are strapped for cash after the first few months, it is highly likely that you will quit your dream and go back to your safe job.

The Money Engine

You're probably asking yourself, "How can I make money for my business when I can't even save a portion of what I earn now?" My initial response would be, "Don't give up on your vision because you lack money to get it going." Your vision should be so large that you cannot accomplish it on your own efforts. If God gave it to you, He will put things in place to bring it to pass. The only requirement is that you show up, do your part, and do it well. If you really want to succeed, you will have to make sacrifices with your time and change your spending habits.

I recall reading an article about a five employee computer software company that was seeking investors to fund their "game-changing" software methodology. For nearly two years, they had been turned down by one investor after the other. They were making money on licensing, but it was not enough to launch into the deep. If one client did not pay on time, salaries and bills would be delayed. The owner was constantly stressed trying to get more license deals while tweaking his million dollar portion of the existing software. He had enthusiastic and talented employees, but they were getting discouraged about the lack of company funding and their late paychecks.

One night, the owner was sitting in his office trying to balance the bank statement. He realized that no matter how he moved things around personally and within the company, he was still $4,000 short of what he needed for the month. Instead of allowing himself to be defeated, he scoured the internet to find the best deal on a two-day retreat for himself and his employees. He found one. Everyone was stunned, but they were looking forward to the trip.

Upon arrival, they were escorted to a breathtaking lunch on the beach. The owner began to tell the employees of the company's dire financial position. He assured them that he wasn't throwing in the towel because he knew in his heart this software was invaluable to thousands of companies. He then asked each one of them to think about other skill sets they had that they could offer to current and new customers while they maintained their current responsibilities. One woman said she was a great web designer in college and that she could design websites in her spare time. Another employee said that he is a self-trained software auditor and that he could offer that service. A third employee offered to provide computer training to community organizations that had funding for such services. He added that he realized that it would not make as much money as his colleagues, yet the extra money could be used to help with the daily operating expenses.

Within four months, the additional services generated revenue for the company equal to their current licensing fees. Customers were satisfied with their standard software offering, so that when the company approached them about additional services, they were eager to sign up. Most signed contracts and paid in advance to hold their completion dates several months later. Now that they were operating in the black, they could hire more employees and increase the service offering. This new revenue generation was bound to attract investors. So the moral of the story is, don't give up! Everything that you need is right in your hand or within your possession; like when God asked Moses, "What is that in your hand?" (Exodus 4:2).

Seek and You Will Find

Often times when you want something bad enough you have to ask for it. Asking is a humbling experience. Many people fail to ask because they are embarrassed or they believe others will think less of them. If you have an idea worth investing in, and it is really too good to be true, you may have to ask others to come alongside you with financial support. Some may just give you a donation with no strings attached. Others may want to be a part of the company. Use prudence in determining the funding model and ownership status before you approach anyone.

There are other ways to obtain funding and the more creative you are, the better your chances of reaching your goal. Really consider building your own sweat equity to earn additional money to set aside for your business. Today, there appears to be a crowdfunding bandwagon. Research it and see if it will be right for you. More traditional ways include getting a line of credit with 60-day payment terms as opposed to the standard 30-day term, or apply for a bank loan. The key is to keep your debt to a minimum before your business is flowing. In addition, many start-ups have been successful using business incubators who help companies achieve early growth by speeding up the process of securing funding, training employees, marketing and providing other critical business services.

In order to know how much money you need to both start-up and transition from your career to your calling, you must first be able to answer these 5 keys questions:

1. What do I sell or want to sell? (Product or Service)
2. Who will I sell it to? (Target Market)
3. How will I sell it? (Sales & Distribution)
4. How will they know about it? (Marketing)
5. What do I need to do to grow my business? (Business Development)

Real numbers don't lie. There are tons of different fixed and variable costs associated with each of these questions. Also consider:

- Will you be a home-based business or will you have a physical location?
- Do you want to focus your efforts locally, regionally, nationally, or globally?
- Will you do traditional print marketing or online?
- Does what you sell require monthly fixed expenses for the tools and systems you need?

There is a lot to think about when it comes to money. While you do not need to have an exact dollar figure or answer to every question at this moment, it gives you an idea of how you should spend your time. Whether you have two hours or 20 hours each week to dedicate to your goals, your time should be spent wisely in the following areas:

- Administrative Tasks (emails, phone calls, etc.)
- Marketing (blogging, podcasting, social media ads etc.)
- Business Development (sales calls, networking meetings)

There may be other functional areas of business you can name that may be specific to your industry. Whatever the additions for your idea, the sure way to make continuous progress is to identify the amount of time you have to spend on your business and then prioritize and schedule your business tasks within that allotted time. It would be beneficial if you created a consistent routine as well. For example, every Wednesday you create social media marketing for the months ahead.

There are two key mistakes that new and aspiring entrepreneurs make when they finally start taking massive action. First, they tend to spend too much time working in their business and not on it. Many startup entrepreneurs spend so much of their time getting ready to get ready. We can give ourselves an allusion that we are working extremely hard on our businesses by creating plans, tweaking plans, and then creating more plans. Being in business is all about an exchange of a product or service for money. Anytime I ever got frustrated in the growth of my business I always ask myself, "Who have I asked today to buy from me?"

Second, your idea is as only as good as your market knows about it. I know your idea is your baby. It's the thing you have been nurturing either in thought or action for some time now. But, don't make the mistake that many people make by keeping it a secret forever. At the end of the day, you desire to be in business to make money. People cannot buy what they do not know exists. Everyone you know should be aware of your new business venture. Not only should they know, but you should also encourage them to spread the word as well. Seek out free advertising often. Use social media to your advantage and attend networking events. At the end of the day, get ready to hustle and work hard, and your efforts will pay off.

COURAGEOUS SPOTLIGHT

FEEDING YOUR NEEDS

Meet Courageous Misty Young, Entrepreneur, Franchise Restaurant Owner, Speaker & Author of Rags to Restaurants

Melissa: Tell me about your start in the restaurant industry? What was your life like before you dared to say, "I want to start this business?"

Misty: I'm going to go back in time to when I was a kid. When I was 11, my parents opened a restaurant in an old ranch town in Southern California. Mom, Dad, Grandma and all six kids lived upstairs in this huge, old ranch house and downstairs we had the restaurant. I was peeling potatoes, bussing tables, serving guests, and going to middle school. I used to think, "I can't wait to get out of this business. It is really hard." But there was also something incredibly, indelibly satisfying about it too. It was real. When you're feeding people in their moment of need, you're meeting them where they are. There was this tug on me that I both liked and didn't like.

I left the family business, got married very young, became a waitress and did restaurant work. I decided I'm really not into this at all. I went to college, got a degree, and went into marketing, public relations, and politics. I became a press secretary to a governor, and attorney general, and worked for a US Senator for a lot of years.

I eventually transitioned into marketing and became the vice president and partner of a marketing agency. In that role, I fell in love with this tiny restaurant in Truckee, CA called The Squeeze Inn. A small hippie place that was 10 feet, 3 inches wide and 62 feet deep. It had 12 tables and 49 chairs.

I had always dreamed of owning this restaurant. My husband and I used to lay in bed and say, "If we could do anything at all, what would it be?" We always said we would own The Squeeze Inn. One day, I asked the owner "How's The Squeeze Inn going? He dropped down kind of low and said, "I love it. I've had it for 26 years. It's great and doing really well." Then he whispered, "I'm thinking of selling it. I haven't put it on the market yet though."

That was it! I didn't hear another word. I made the presentation on autopilot. At the end of the meeting, we all shook hands, I ran back to my office, slammed the door, called my husband and I said, "Oh my gosh, The Squeeze Inn is for sale!" Within 14 hours, I was on the phone making an offer and just a couple months later the deal was done and we took over the business. The scary thing was I didn't want to be in the restaurant business, I wanted to be a businesswoman.

Melissa: What did it take to start the restaurant and how did you know it would work? How did you know "I can turn this around?"

Misty: First off, what does it take to get started? I really knew in my soul, my bones, my skeleton – the universe loves speed. The moment I heard the opportunity was available, I checked it out. I went into "how do I make this happen" mode. Which is why the next morning, I called him. The second thing – how did I know I could turn this around? I believe in me. I really believe in me because I have the full weight, glory, and bounty of the universe behind me to set me up for success. I believe that what I claim and state in fact the universe is obligated to deliver it to me. It may not work in the way I think it's going to work. It may not come in the timing I want, but I know if I stay focused on success, opportunity, and creative ideas the universe finds a way to bring in circumstances, events, people and things to support my goals and dream. I always hold my vision.

I knew that restaurant had potential. It had everything to turn from what it was when I bought it in 2004, one floundering location, to what it is today – five flourishing locations, a 1.5 million-dollar annual payroll, 96 employees across two states, and we're now franchising. We completed the entire legal sweep of everything that has to be done from regulatory and intellectual property, copyrighting materials, and developing platforms and systems. Now we're going to pull the marketing trigger and take this thing national. I could see that, way back then. But if you can see it and hold that vision, it is yours.

Melissa: What's next? Most people would be okay with achieving their dream of owning a restaurant. Tell me about the moment when you knew it was not just about the 62-foot diner, that it was something much bigger.

Misty: It's kind of crazy because at first I was okay with it. When we took over the restaurant, I was extraordinarily fulfilled and highly energetic. And I thought that was it. We leveraged everything we had to make the deal come together. And I was stoked up and working days, nights, weekends, and holidays doing whatever it took to systematize this thing. There was a moment when I realized this could be something bigger. It was after an experience I deemed a failure.

I lost a lot of money, a lot of reputation, and a lot of momentum. In my mind, the other restaurant deal was a big failure. But as I said earlier, the universe is obligated to bring us what we want. Although it may not look like what we think it is. I think the universe protected our family and all the families in the community that depend on us because that other restaurant ended up running into some trouble. But the great thing that came out of it was it opened our minds. We all looked at each other and said, "Wow! If we were able to consider taking on a business three times the volume of what we're doing, what else could we do? Do you think we could open a second location?" That's what started the discussion and what we did next, which was open number two, three, four, and five.

Melissa: It's the whole aspect of learning trial by fire.

Misty: Yes!

Melissa: What are you up to now in addition to the franchising?

Misty: There are three things I am doing. I have this insatiable desire to create economic opportunity. It starts with what's my big picture? My ultimate human dream is I ask the universe every single day, "How may I serve? One of the ways I want to serve, and I called this out a dozen years ago, is I want to give away a million dollars every year. I had no idea how I would get there but now it's all starting to come together to make this happen. I want to serve the universe by serving people and give away a million dollars a year. Now, to do that, you've got to make a million dollars – a lot of money. And you've got to be focused on a big dream and a big vision, and I am.

Melissa: I'm speechless in reference to who you are as a person, the vision you have inside of you, and what you decided to do to see it come to fruition. Thank you.

Filling a need is every entrepreneur's dream. In Misty's case, she is feeding both a natural appetite for her customers with creative and tasty breakfast and lunch menu options, while feeding her employees with love and respect, like members of the family. Using keen business sense and evaluating what works and what doesn't, has paved the way for Misty's success at the Squeeze Inn. Don't get so caught up with size in wanting to open the biggest restaurant on your side of town. A major factor in Misty's franchise success is keeping her restaurants small, quaint, with a down-home feel. Be willing to do what works for you and your business instead of keeping up with everyone else's.

INVESTING IN YOURSELF

"Formal education will make you a living; self-education will make you a fortune."
JIM ROHN

I have admired John Maxwell's work all my life. He is often referred to as the #1 leadership expert in the world. When I researched the opportunity to be a part of his coaching and teaching team, my heart skipped a beat or two. All I wanted to know were two things: the core requirements and how much it cost. Of course, the process was set up so that the two key pieces of information I needed were not available online. The only way to get my answer was through a program coordinator.

I remember listening to the coordinator share about all the value I would get with the program and braced myself for the price tag. While the investment was significantly less than what I had anticipated, it was still *way* more than I had ever paid for a personal investment, outside of traditional formal education. It was the kind of price tag that makes you take a big gulp, a deep breath, and sleep on it a night or two before you click the "Enroll Now" button. However, there was something deep down inside of me that knew if I was really going to take the leap and start my purpose driven transition once and for all, I needed to click the button. To date, it was the best click that I have made.

For me, it marked a transition and turning point in my life. One where I finally took my growth and development into my own hands. I no longer left it up to the companies I worked for, maneuvering within their finicky budgets, or whether or not they thought I had enough potential to be a part of the best personal development programs in the country. I took matters into my own hands.

> *"Jim, if you want to be wealthy and happy, learn this lesson well: learn to work harder on yourself than you do on your job."*
> JOHN EARL SHOAFF (JIM ROHN'S MENTOR)

Most people try to go through their journey alone. Others look into personal development opportunities, only to get sticker shocked and revert back to going it alone. A few take the jump and go all in, with no questions asked. What is your future worth to you? I cannot tell you how many times I've kicked myself for not acting fast enough. After forgoing thousands of dollars, I have learned not to procrastinate on learning opportunities I know will take me to my next level. I remember my desire to attend a four-day conference. When registration first opened I hesitated for two reasons: i) The $697 early bird registration investment, and ii) I was double-booked two of the four days.

I didn't register at that time. Instead, I watched and I waited, knowing deep down in my heart that I wanted to be there but let the deadlines pass. Finally, on the last day of registration, something within me said, "Melissa you have to be there, even if it is to only to attend for one day and watch the rest virtually." I ended up paying the full registration of the conference, a whopping $1697! That's not a typo, a whole *thousand dollars more*! But I knew it was time for me to stop procrastinating and jump in.

After two years of attending coaching conferences and training, my speaking fee increased by thousands of dollars. Investing in my gift, showing up, and being in the room with the right people, gave me the confidence and additional knowledge to make the next leap. This mindset shift was pivotal to my success. It was the difference between an *investor mindset* of investing in myself, versus a complacent mindset of sitting back and waiting for personal growth to miraculously happen on its own.

WALKING OUT STEP #7

Let's face it, if you don't invest in yourself, chances are no one else will. If you were fortunate to take advantage of your corporate-funded development opportunities then that's great. You probably got comfortable in an environment of high-potential leaders traveling around on someone else's dime. Have you developed an entitlement mindset that growth opportunities should be given to you? If so, you must immediately undergo a mindset shift as you are *now* responsible for your own progress and success.

Many of my clients were just like me when I first left Corporate America. They had never invested in themselves and had not worked with a coach. The thought of the investment caused that familiar internal tension that one experiences when leaving his or her comfort zone. It is from wanting to move forward, but spending that much money causes hesitation and maybe even heartburn. Trust me, you are worth it.

Counting up the costs is just as critical as taking the first step and saying "Yes!" It requires a serious effort and commitment to researching and writing the vision, creating funding opportunities, changing your spending habits, and investing in yourself. Take a moment to consider where you stand in the following areas:

1. Have you been financially responsible? Request a copy of your credit score to ensure its accuracy and begin taking action to fix errors. Your personal credit history will become a factor if you desire a line of credit or a bank loan.
2. Do you have an understanding of business finance? Can you create a balance sheet? Enroll in a general financial accounting course to give you a basic understanding of appropriate recordkeeping. Hire an accountant to handle your financial affairs.
3. What "after work" services can you provide today to jumpstart your business funding?
4. Have you made a list of potential business mentors? Seek someone whom you admire that has successfully taken the leap.

5. Have you researched the SBA (Small Business Administration) and other business assistance programs? There are several reputable start-up organizations to help you regardless of where you are in the process.

By Any Means Necessary

We all know that moving from your career to your calling does not just *happen*. It is a journey that only few will take. One where even fewer will get the support they need to ensure true success. Those that succeed adopt a "by any means necessary" mindset. They have made an unbreakable commitment with themselves that they will stay true to their dreams *by any means necessary*. That includes taking the right steps to invest in themselves and their future.

Reflections and Learnings

_____

_____

_____

_____

_____

_____

_____

_____

_____

_____

_____

_____

_____

_____

_____

_____

_____

_____

COURAGEOUS STEP #8

WHO'S ON YOUR TEAM?

"The best support system is having people in your life who love and praise you one minute and check you the next."

Your inner circle can be comprised of your best friend, people in your family, and those that you have met along the way. However, at least one of those people needs to be someone who you totally trust to speak truths to you that no one else has the guts to say. You will also need a person to help guide and show you the way, especially if they have been there before. That person is often a mentor or coach. We all need someone to give us that outside perspective in order to see things clearly, even a coach like me.

I have watched inspirational speaker, Lisa Nichols, talk about the first time meeting Oprah. Of all the things they could have talked about, the first question they were dying to ask each other was, "Who's your coach?" Both of them are powerful women in their own right, with extremely close friends. Yet as two successful experts in their fields, they both realized the importance of support from others.

"You need an external viewpoint to help you see things from the right perspective!"

Having an external perspective is what gives you the strength and inspiration to keep going on your hardest days. It gives you the confidence to stand up taller and know your value when your mind tells you there is no way you can charge that much. If you lack confidence in your abilities, others will see it as well. No one will ever sign a contract with a person exhibiting a fear-based attitude.

I once asked a coaching client who kept him motivated and accountable in his inner circle. He said, "No one. My dreams are so big that most people can't understand them and think I'm crazy!" He's exactly right. That is why you have to surround yourself with dreamers, visionaries, and go-getters, just like yourself. Even within that circle, you are the only one who God has tasked with your specific vision.

So, now it's your turn to answer, "Who's on your team?" Who can you count on, connect and strategize with? For me, I have a team of special people in my life who I absolutely could not thrive without. True potential cannot be reached through your own efforts, strengths, abilities, or knowledge. It can only happen in conjunction with others.

The catch is when we allow ourselves to dream about a life that seems unreachable. We can get so overwhelmed with seemingly unrealistic thoughts. They can keep us from mentioning it to anyone else, sometimes not even our spouse or closest friends. If it sounds crazy to us, it has to be crazy to them too, right? Two minds limited in thinking equals limited outcomes. That is why you have to expand your circle!

Your circle must include people that believe in you and can also see further than you when your vision gets blurry. Especially when things are not working as you expected or you want to give up. If you are currently a corporate leader, consider this question:

"Do you have the team you want and need?
If not, are you willing to do something about?"

Now this same question applies to you. When you look at your team list above, is it your ideal team? Not just limited to names and people, but also the characteristics and qualities you need in a powerhouse team.

Characteristics and Qualities of a Powerhouse Team:

As important as a support system is, most people do not have one. I was shocked, when running a CEO Mastermind for one of my corporate clients, that even though each of the business owners had thriving businesses, they had no one to strategize with outside of their immediate employees. Each had the desire, but had not taken the time to build meaningful relationships outside of their companies.

In John Maxwell's #1 best-selling book, *The 21 Irrefutable Laws of Leadership,* he essentially explains a concept called, *The Law of the Lid.* It shows that our potential will never be able to exceed our own ability. If our leadership ability is at a 6, on a scale of 1 to 10, our potential will never exceed a 6. The only way that we ever reach our full potential is if we "raise the lid" on our abilities, which only comes through growth and development.

Sure, it might seem hard to find so many exceptional qualities in one person, but transparency and vulnerability will create space for the right people to appear at the right time. As life-changers, dreamers, and visionaries, we have to be willing to be vulnerable, trust others, take risks, and share thoughts we kept so closely guarded.

Dear Friend: You're Fired!

The best thing you can ever do when making a leap of this kind, is to fire your friends. Did I just say that? Absolutely! I do not really mean fire your friends completely – they are one of our best assets in life. Some of my best conversations about life are with my closest friends. However, in certain seasons we accidentally hire them as our counselors, coaches, mentors, trainers, nutrition experts, etc. We become dependent on their opinions, asking questions like:

- What do you think about this?
- How would you feel?
- What would you do?
- What would you say?
- What do you think I should do?

Sound familiar? There is absolutely nothing wrong with getting their feedback. However, you also run the risk of them jumping out of the "advisor role" and simply just being your friend. You know, like the time you guys just finished having an intense conversation about how you are both going to get in shape, but opt to go for dessert right after the conversation. Again, friends are necessary, but don't confuse your friends that I discuss in the latter Chapter 10, Who's Riding Shotgun?, with those on your core business building team. Your "shotgun" friends are those that help you escape from your business mindset and daily challenges, and encourage you let loose and have fun.

How Do I Build a Team?

My inner circle is built of amazing relationships, both new and old. You would be surprised at who God sends your way to speak life into you. It could be someone you have only known for a short amount of time or forever. The growth of those you can entrust your dreams with evolves over time.

True visionaries love to work with those who are not just talking the talk, but walking the walk. When I am surrounded by people who are complainers, procrastinators, extremely fearful, or full of excuses, I make a conscious decision to pull back. Then I identify those that are more like myself; ready to change the world, or at least a small piece of it.

Keys to building the right team:

1. **Do not be afraid to pull back** or let go of people who do not deserve to be in your most sacred place – where your dreams and plans reside.

2. **Take the time to build relationships.** Everyone can tell the moment they meet a person if they are going to connect. You can tell if the two of you have kindred spirits and if it is something beyond the networking opportunity. I have met several of my closest friends and supporters at networking events. I knew within five minutes that we were supposed to meet and stay connected as we grew in life and business. What opportunities are you missing out on by not letting others in?

3. **Identify people you admire and ASK.** It is hard to find people with the same amount of drive I have. My eyes light up and I take notice when I see someone who is just as serious and moving with similar momentum to their dreams. I remember watching a Facebook friend from afar who I knew was moving and grooving just like I was. We had similar styles when it came to our work and had taken a five-week course together previously. Knowing I wanted to be associated with more game-changers, I sent her a message letting her know I would love to connect and start strategizing with her. To my surprise, she had been thinking the same thing about me! Who can you reach out to to begin a new relationship with today?

4. **SHARE.** I know everyone will not understand your dreams and the risks you are willing to take. However, the right people cannot inspire, encourage, or believe in what they do not know. No, not everyone will be excited and jump on board to the dream God has placed inside of you. But that does not mean there are not others that have been specifically assigned to your life who will. Who do you need to be more transparent with about your goals and dreams?

5. **Support others.** I learned from my writing coach, Kary Oberbrunner, author of Day Job to Dream Job, the more you help others achieve their dreams, the more they will help you achieve yours. Whose goals and dreams are you supporting? As you help to build other people's platform yours will be built as well.

WALKING OUT STEP #8

We often start down the path to our dreams like a lone ranger. We believe that we are the only ones who can get things done and we shut others out. As we face challenges, which are inevitable, we realize that we were not supposed to do everything on our own. It's OK to be vulnerable and share your thoughts and dreams. There are people waiting to provide the emotional, spiritual, relational, and even financial support that you need.

PART IV

Determine Your Staying Power (The Why)

COURAGEOUS STEP #9

ARE YOU A QUITTER?

"Your mind can't be in two places at one time. Are you planning for your success? Or you are planning for your failure?"

et's be honest. There are days when you are not going to feel up to the grind. If you have not experienced it yet, you will. You will feel emotional, incapable, less than, irrelevant, unnoticed, and like nothing is working at times. You may also feel like everyone else is ahead of you. But just like you cannot base the status of your life on how you feel at the moment, you also cannot associate it with the pursuit of your calling.

One day, I received an inquiry that I am sure many of you can relate to:

"Hello Melissa,

I'm in the process of pursuing my dreams but I'm having difficulty stay-ing strong and focused. There have been all kinds of obstacles in my way. My question is, how do you stay strong and focused when there are many obstacles in your way?

Thanks"

I am sure you have asked yourself this question a time or two. Even when the answer is "no,' not right now, no response, or when there is only one person in the audience, you ultimately get stronger each time, regardless of the obstacle. I will never forget sitting in my office in July of 2013, the month before I got laid off. I already knew that my time was almost up in my corporate career. It was not because I thought a layoff was coming. It was because I said to myself, "I can always go back to corporate if it does not work out." I don't feel like this anymore. Like my old self, most of you have carved a way out in your minds to pack up and go back to your old career if the dream does not work out.

Today, going back is not an option. I learned that I could not live with one foot inside the door of my dream and the other foot ready to run at the slightest sign of danger. Write this on a PostIt note, "There is no Plan B." That essentially means you cannot quit. Will plans have to change or be tweaked? Yes. But as long as they are moving you towards the very thing that you want to do, instead of away from it, start reworking them.

It has to come to the point when a hard day is literally just that, a hard day. Not a day that you quit. Being called to something means you are drawn to it, that there is space specifically for you, and an impact only you are supposed to make. It is a realization that your mere existence and fulfillment in life is dependent upon you walking out this journey. That fulfillment cannot happen if you are always looking back or willing to make a U-turn at the first obstacle you face.

One Friday morning, I received a coaching inquiry. During my intake conversation with the potential client that afternoon, she said, "I've been following you and I reached out because I feel like I'm about to give up!" She was having a hard day, frustrated because she wasn't sure what to do next, and discouraged because she wasn't seeing any fruit for the labor she had already put in. I encouraged her that there was no need to panic as this was a typical experience for aspiring and new entrepreneurs.

The next thing we talked about was how she had to take the "Q" word out of her vocabulary. If this leap was something she really felt "called" to do, quitting could not be an option. That's it folks, the end of story. If you believe you are called to do something, then do it. If it is not working as well as you would like, or you do not have the momentum you desire, take those needs back to the person who gave you the calling in the first place – God. His word says, "Call to me and I will answer you and show you great and mighty things!" (Jeremiah 33:3).

*And He said to me, "My grace is sufficient for you, for
My strength is made perfect in weakness." Therefore
most gladly I will rather boast in my infirmities,
that the power of Christ may rest upon me.
- 2 CORINTHIANS 12:9*

You have to know there will be days that you will have to sacrifice in order to achieve the success and significance you believe God has destined for your life. There is no way you can continuously look back and work on your future at the same time. The very thing that God has called you to do will also require surrender and submission to the process. The quickest way to stay where you are is to be unwilling to change your mundane routines for radical commitment and consistency.

More than likely, you will find the journey to be much harder than you have ever thought. Often, God only allows us to experience what we need in the moment to get us to the next step. Many of us would never dare to sign up if we truly knew what lies ahead. We have to know that the vision God placed in our heart is not only possible, but meant to be. We are supposed to hold on to the vision, walk by faith, and persevere until it comes to pass.

*"The process is just as important as your purpose.
Foregoing the process means you will be ill-
equipped for your purpose!"*

COURAGEOUS SPOTLIGHT

WORTH FOLLOWING

Meet Courageous Dr. Jen Bennett
Social Media Expert, Social Media Specialist, Author, and Speaker

M: Tell us what you were doing before you became a social media expert and how you transitioned into social media.

J: Before social media and life coaching, I was in education full-time. I was working as a high school English teacher and a school administrator at a private school. I was in education for about eight years. I had the opportunity to work in both public and private schools. Before that, I was in youth ministry full-time. And I'll tell you, if you would have told me in 1999, when I was getting my master's degree at seminary I would end up doing social media full-time, I would have laughed. My heart was set on going into ministry full-time and I did. I worked at a church in Texas and in Miami. From there, God led me into education. From education, God led me home to start building my life coaching business, and then all of a sudden, social media popped up. I absolutely fell in love with it. I still laugh at the transition because I honestly thought I was going to end up staying in education for a while.

M: A lot of twists and turns in your career to get to this point. What was the biggest thing that peeked your interest in social media?

J: It's interesting. When I was doing ministry full-time as a youth minister, I ended up deeply wounded by the church, by some of the people there, and the leadership. When I left the church, God opened up an opportunity for me to get into education and eventually, a private school. I thought that is where God was going to keep me. I was teaching, in leadership, and I was at a private school where I had the opportunity to pour into the lives of these students, just like I did when I was doing youth ministry. In my mind, even though some of my dreams felt like they disappeared because of what happened with the church, I felt like God was saying, "Okay, I don't want you working in the church right now. I want you to be in education.

In 2011, I started feeling this nudge to come home. I had just had a baby. My son was a year old and I desired to spend more time with him. And, of course, all the typical questions popped up in my mind. "How are we going to make this work? What happens if we can't pay our bills? What happens if we lose our home?" All of those fears were creeping in, but deep down inside, I felt like God was saying to me, "Jen, trust me. This is what I want you to do. Trust me, give your notice. It's time for you to come home." So, I did. I knew God was telling me to even though I had more questions than answers. It was a faith test, because for so many years, I had shared about trusting God. "Trust in God. Put your faith in God." And here it was, another opportunity in my life where God was saying, "Okay, Jen. You've been talking about this to your students, are you really going to trust Me?"

At the time when I was pursuing my life coaching business, social media came up and the coach I was working with offered a social media manager's training course. As I looked into it, I was like, "Hmm! This might be interesting!" I really loved social media and had developed some great relationships with women online. God allowed me to use social media to speak life into the hearts of these women to encourage them. So I took the course on a whim to see what it was like and I instantly fell in love even more. I felt it was the direction God was leading me into. January of 2012 is when I took that step and honestly, I haven't looked back. I love this and I see where God has taken all of my hopes, dreams, and desires I had and put it into this role in social media. I would have never thought He would have done it this way.

M: That's an amazing story. And your influence has been expanded. It's not just for a group or for a church, but it's technically the world. A lot of times we have our dreams, and they seem good at the time, but they are small in comparison to what He has for us.

J: Exactly! It continues to amaze me how God works in every little detail. One of my most favorite books is called *The Three Trees*. It is an amazing book and I used it when I did life coaching with women. It is a story of three trees who had hopes and dreams for their lives. Before they knew it, their hopes and dreams were crushed. One tree wanted to be the tallest tree in the forest – so that whenever people would look at it, they would immediately think of God because the tree was pointing to God. But this tree all of a sudden found itself being chopped down. And the tree was like, "Oh my goodness! What just happened to my goals and dreams?" And then later on, this one specific tree realized that it was being used to create the manger that Jesus would lay in. I love it because it's such a clear picture of how we have certain goals and dreams. Much like this tree who wanted to be the tallest tree in the forest so whenever people looked at it, it would always remind people of God. And yet, it went through this process where it thought, "My dreams have died."

For many of us, sometimes that happens and we're like, "What's going on? This isn't the way I wanted my life to turn out." When we get to the other side, we realize God has not taken our goals and dreams, but used them in another way we would have never imagined, much like this tree. This tree was now holding baby Jesus and whenever people saw the manger or saw pictures of baby Jesus at Christmas, they would always think of Jesus. I think that's what God does with us. He takes our hopes and dreams. We have our plans but God takes us through a process and shows us how He's using those dreams in ways we would have never imagined.

M: That's a great analogy everyone can relate to. What would you tell women who are looking to take the next step into a new season?

J: The biggest thing is I had to come to a point where I knew in my heart God was calling me to take a step of faith. I had to realize and come to terms with the fact that I would not have all the answers up front. For many of us, that is something that holds us back from pursuing the calling, the career, or what it is God is calling us to. We want all of the answers up front. We want a perfectly laid out plan. We want to know how it's going to look. And I came to realize that's not the way God works. Many times, He wants us to take a step and then when we take that step, He'll show us the next step, and the next step after that. I had a friend reach out to me. She said, "I know God's calling me to do such and such." And I said, "Well, what's holding you back?" She said, "Comfort." That is another big thing we have to come to terms with. Sometimes, when God's calling us to take a step or to move in new direction, we don't want to get uncomfortable. We know that taking that step would make us uncomfortable.

M: We often don't step out, we hesitate, delay, or go back to what was comfortable, instead of being willing to be like Peter did in the Bible and step out onto the water. He was told, "Keep your eyes on me." But that statement is not easy in our scariest situations.

J: Exactly. I love that example of Peter. Many times, God is like, "Just focus on me. Watch me. Watch what I will do." It's when we take our eyes off of that focus, take our eyes off of Him and what He's doing in our lives we start to sink. If we can focus on Him and that one step He's asking us to take, He promises us to never leave us or forsake us. He promises to always be there so we know He's calling us to something. We just have to take that jump.

My new book is going to explore the topic of being worth following. It's going to have insight into social media, but what I love about it, is that it's going to have some insight about life. It's not a book where I'm telling you, "Here's a great app, use this to gain more followers!" It's more about becoming a person, a business, an organization, a church, or ministry. Someone that is worth following on social media so that ultimately you can make a bigger impact for the kingdom. My goal is to have it completed and out by next year. I've received some great encouragement from people who tell me they're ready to read it. I'm excited to get the "be worth following" message out there and share it with many.

Imagine if Dr. Jen Bennett quit seeking out her purpose because of hurt feelings in a prior organization? Once you come to grips that everyone is not going to like you or have your best interest at heart, you will not let negative words or actions stop you from moving forward. Quitting is the easiest thing you can do. Finding new solutions and opportunities is hard. At the end of the day, you should be pursuing something worth fighting for, so you can become someone worth following.

The 20-Minute Pity Party™
The 20-Minute Praise Party™

It is impossible to quit the pursuit of your calling. It will continue to nag and follow you until you see full manifestation. This pursuit is not just for the organized, the sophisticated, the super faithful, the highly educated, or talented. It is for those that not only sense something greater, but believe with every fiber of their being that they have arrived at this awesome place and waiting to hear God's voice to make the next move.

Everyone's starting point and journey is different. Don't get discouraged as you compare your level of success to someone else's. Constant comparison will always keep you feeling like you are left behind, unable to celebrate how far you've come. OK I really get it. You want to quit because:

- There are times when you feel like it is too hard.
- There are times that you think you are not good enough.
- There are times when you feel like you do not know enough people, have enough resources, nor know enough to make a difference.

Guess what? I've been there and done that! There truly is a light at the end of the tunnel, which I have finally experienced by throwing myself a 20-minute Pity Party™. You may be thinking, "Throw myself a what, Melissa?" But it is so liberating to have a moment to scream, cry, question yourself, your life, and then release it. One of my best friends once told me, it's ok to cry just as long as you don't stay there. Numerous studies have shown that a mere 20 minutes of a routine activity can truly benefit your overall health. For example, the National Sleep Foundation recommends 20-30 minute naps to improve alertness and performance. Over the years, I have come across several medical journals that mention the effectiveness of a 20-minute workout each day. Also, studies on patients with high blood pressure, depression, heart attack and stroke, who meditated 20 minutes, twice a day, showed improvement.

Here are a few things that you can do in your 20-Minute Pity Party™ that will eventually turn things around, to make room for your all out dance and shout, 20-Minute Praise Party™:

- Set a timer
- It's OK to cry, shout, and let out your feelings of being overwhelmed or stagnant.
- Recite your favorite scripture
- Mediate on scripture or just meditate in silence/stillness
- Take a nap
- Afterwards, make a list of things that triggered the pity moment and schedule time to discuss with your mentor or trusted business advisor.

After engaging in several of these exercises, you will be surprised how they will become few and far between. It's normal to feel the way you do, but don't get stuck in pity. As my grandmother would say, "don't wallow in it." Remember, the goal is to turn your 20-Minute Pity Party™ into your 20-Minute Praise Party™!   As you release what is getting in your way, you begin to make room for what you have and where you are going.   Make it a time of thanks and gratitude.   Think and reflect on everything that is happening in your favor. Everything counts.   In fact, why don't you try it right now and see if it doesn't change your countenance? After you get those negative thoughts and emotions out of your system, you will be closer than you've ever been.

Doing Your part

Before you think of quitting or engaging in a pity party, "Have you done all that you can do?" This is the question I ask my clients often, especially in times of extreme frustration. Nearly every response is, "*no.*"

- Have you called everyone you know?
- Have you followed-up with everyone you've called at least 7-10 times?
- Have you been relentless in everything you were supposed to do for the day?

I could keep adding to the list of questions, but the answer to these questions and more, is likely a resounding *"no."* The only people who quit are those who try to operate in their calling while they are still in their comfort zone. You cannot do both. It's impossible. In my industry, I often think that if I have not contacted every university, every corporation, nor have I followed up relentlessly, I have no excuse to quit! The math is simple: $0 + 0 = 0$. In other words, minimal effort = minimal results. Even if you think you have done everything, I am going to challenge you to think some more, pray some more, and wake up with a fresh start tomorrow. There are always some unturned rocks to discover.

Most people look at the success of others and want to be there today. But can I tell you a little secret? There are no overnight successes! I know it may seem that way sometimes, but I encourage you to do your homework. The next person you see on your social media timeline who seems to be excelling in the very thing you want to do, look them up. You will see who they are and what they have become is not new, only new to you. They put time and work into it. The same fundamental level of grit and grind just like everyone else.

In the age of social media and phone apps, things happen faster every single day. One tweet or instagram post can make the most unlikely person an overnight success. A viral post can have someone sitting in their living room one day, content with their ordinary life, and suddenly thrust them on every major news network the next day. The speed of their success still comes with pain, sacrifice, and discomfort down the line. Everything that you are experiencing now in the beginning, they too will experience along the way, but in the public eye.

In our pity moments, we are being processed. The pain we would much rather avoid is grooming us for our future. The ability to realize this concept puts you in a position to not only keep going, but learn how to turn your challenges into amazing success stories.

One of my biggest pet peeves is when coaches and mentors essentially promise people overnight success. Everyone has found *the best* formula to launch your business, change your career, and make a six-figure income (sometimes seven), while running your business part-time and vacationing on an extravagant island. Is it possible? I believe so. But I would dare to ask,

"How many attempts? How many years? How many business models?" These are key questions to uncover what they really went through to achieve that level of success. It is such a misrepresentation. All the while, they are preying on the novice entrepreneur who desperately wants to achieve that kind of success by putting in a few hours work.

Courage is a Repetitive Action

The key to your longevity is doing the right things over and over again daily, relentlessly, whether you like them or not. There were activities in my business early on that I did not see as income-producing at first, like social media or blogging. I went back forth on my levels of consistency because I did not see the immediate return. Even though I did not see it, it still needed to be done. I created routines, and checklists until I started to get more consistent over time.

I am thankful that *courage* is my driving force most days. That is, until I encountered other things along my path that scared me, like cold-calling people on the phone or bracing myself for hearing the word "no." One morning I woke up dreading the sales calls I had to make. Like most people, I hated not getting an answer, and leaving a voicemail. This was when I had not quite gotten the hang of it. I secretly hoped that people would just call me instead, based on my social media marketing. I was wrong. Once I started writing out different scripts to handle different rejections or excuses, I became better at it, and my preparation paid off.

At times, doing tasks over and over may seem pointless or feel like they do not yield any results. There are all kinds of examples I can share about this, like when I committed to doing a social media strategy, but did not really see the numbers grow at first. Or when I decided to make sure to send my newsletter and post on my blog consistently, but did not really see my email list grow. There were so many other things that would often make me feel like I was doing everything right, but not seeing any results. It can be the most frustrating and daunting place to be – feeling like you are giving something your **all**, but not seeing the outcomes you desire or need to see from your work. Taking a leap to walk in your calling is an ongoing learning process that comes with seemingly insurmountable odds that only the strong can survive.

WALKING OUT STEP #9

Since quitting is not an option, nor is going back to your comfortable, yet unfulfilling job, you have no choice but to hold you head up, stick your chest out, and get with the program that was designed specifically for you. It's OK to have days of unproductiveness, doubt, and fear, but it's NOT OK to get stuck there. Give yourself time to let go of those insecure moments with the 20-Minute Pity Party™. After your 20 minutes are up, you should go about your day with a new mindset and tenacity. Over time, you will see how your pity party has transformed into your praise party.

Before having your pity party, write out the following:

1. What can you do differently *today* that will take an ounce of stress off?
2. What can you do differently *tomorrow* that will take an ounce of stress off?
3. Is there someone you can enlist to help you with one aspect of your business on a weekly, bi-weekly, or monthly basis?

Remember, some days will be better than others. There are no guarantees that you will have more good days than bad ones. Try not to put so much pressure on yourself to complete certain tasks in a few hours or a few days. The saying, "Rome wasn't built in a day" comes to mind when I hear clients ready to give up before they really gain traction. If this is what you were called to do, believe it with all your heart, yet know that it will take time. Eliminate the "Q" word from your vocabulary now!

Reflections and Learnings

_____

_____

_____

_____

_____

_____

_____

"I hated every minute of training, but I said,
"Don't quit. Suffer now and live the
rest of your life as a champion."
-MUHAMMAD ALI

COURAGEOUS STEP #10
Who's Riding Shotgun?

> *"Lots of people want to ride with you in the limo,*
> *but what you want is someone who will take the*
> *bus with you when the limo breaks down."*
> *-Oprah Winfrey*

The transition to leaping from your career to your calling can put an emotional strain on your relationships. Many people embark upon the biggest adventure of their lives expecting those in their closest circle to automatically come along for the ride. Then they are disappointed when some of them not only do not come alongside us, but they don't even ask about it, nor inquire about what help or resources they can provide. Actually, take heart in knowing that you don't need every friend and family member to be concerned about your business. Rather, you need them to be there to help take your mind off the business and invite you to engage in activities that put fun and laughter in your heart.

Another flashback before officially leaving Corporate America, is when I was determined to plan my first event. I set a date, found the cutest venue that held 25 people, and started marketing. It was exactly what I wanted: a creative environment at a spa, including a mini-training from me, and mini-spa services. As an added perk, I gave my participants various teas, champagnes, and scrumptious food! All for a whopping $97. In my eyes, it was already a sold out event! I mean, what an amazing experience, full of so much value! I instantly thought that marketing was going to be a cinch. Who wouldn't want to be there? Besides, I knew at least 25 friends and family members, so of course it would be a full event. I started my marketing campaign and received two registrations in the beginning.

As the registration deadline drew closer, I started getting nervous. I had just six registrations, but began to worry that no one else would register or show up to the event. However, my worry turned into anger as I began to count the number of friends and family members who had not registered or even mentioned trying to attend. As one of my friends, and an aspiring entrepreneur, once said about her own dream, "Didn't they know this was my dream? Didn't they know how much I was putting into this and how much it meant to me?"

Even though all of that was true, registrations still remained stagnant. I can remember feeling deeply hurt. Why wouldn't they want to support me? Why wouldn't they just come? In the end, I had 12 women register – half of the number I originally planned. Even with half the number, the experience turned out better than I planned. It was amazing! It was simultaneously as much of a learning experience for me as it was an overall awesome experience for everyone else.

I have learned so much about event planning and launching programs since then. However, it still does not overshadow the fact that we often blindly go into our own ventures with the expectation that everyone who is important to us is going to ride along with us. Remember, you don't need everyone connected to you to ride along for your business venture. I remember hearing a speaker once share that we are often upset at the people who do not support our dream that we lose sight of the fact that it is OUR dream and not theirs. Just because *you* finally got a hold of your calling, it does not mean that everyone else is supposed run with it too.

Before you get to the end of your journey, there will be people around you that you did not know before you started. People so supportive, you would have never expected them to be there for you, since you've only known them for a short amount of time. On the other hand, there will be those that are missing from your photo op that you *never* thought would be watching from afar. They weren't supposed to.

I have the majority of the same friendships I did when I first started. The relationships did not go away, but the dynamics and my expectations of some of those friends had to shift. I learned I could not project my purpose, passion, love for what I was doing, or even my most painful moments on them. Just because I ate, drank, slept, and thought about my crazy ideas all the time, did not mean they did too. I learned that when they did not ask about it, it did not mean that they loved me any less. It just meant that they had their own priorities in life and I had mine. I also had to learn that going on the most adventurous faith walk of my life, was my *own* walk, not theirs.

You will learn what conversations to have with different kinds of people. You will know who will understand the ins and outs of your day, who can provide valuable insight, and who can't. You will also be able to take comfort in the highs and lows of your experiences with sincere support, without judgement, and with prayer.

Along your journey, God will show you answers to:

- The people who will be relentlessly praying for you.
- The people you should be closely connected to so you can be a lifeline to each other.
- The people who will be supporting you from the sidelines but sending good vibes your way.
- Those you need to let go.

Unfriended

A real wake-up call for me was when I saw a Facebook picture of close corporate friends I used to hang out with at a non-corporate outing. It felt weird looking at the picture, especially since I wasn't in it! A tinge of sadness came over me when it hit me that I was not invited. It was the first of many encounters and disappointments along the journey of my entrepreneurial pursuit where I had to realize that in groups where I was previously an insider, I was now an outsider. I had to learn to trust that God would send the people I needed when I needed them.

"Trust that God will send you who and
what you need when you need it!"

There are countless examples of people I have met along my journey who are definite connections from God. They came and inserted themselves into my life like they had been there all along. Do not allow yourself to miss the blessing right in front of you by continuously looking back at disappointments concerning who is not riding with you. There are too many blessings to count from the people who have crossed my path to date whether it was for a season or for a lifetime. Discover the relentless desire to ride with whomever He leads you to. You don't have to settle for sitting in the back seat with your old friend who makes you feel like you are stuck wearing tight shoes!

WALKING OUT STEP #10

Prayer Warriors

One of the key elements essential to my personal success, is the small team of people who constantly pray for me. Many of whom took it upon themselves to do so because we have that type of connection. They know the desires of my heart and the gifts that reside within me. It is without fail, that I will get a text on the day of a speaking engagement from several of them saying they are praying for me that day. Many times, I have been so busy, that I did not get a chance to remind them – they simply remembered and prayed for me. God began to assign people to my life to encourage, support, and pray for me. Not a lot of people, but just enough to keep me going when I needed it most. Every calling comes with both a promise and a burden. Both promises and burdens must be dealt with and nurtured in prayer.

COURAGEOUS STEP #11

ARE YOU CHICKEN?

"Fear can become so real that people give it guest privileges in their hearts and homes."

A huge obstacle that stops budding dreamers is FEAR! Whether it is the fear of success, fear of failure, or fear of what others will think, are all blockers to achieving your goals. Fear can be a debilitating emotion. A second challenge is ISOLATION. Being connected brings energy and sparks momentum. However, the best way to slow yourself down is to entertain and experience aloneness for too long.

One morning, I shared this post on social media about some of my own thoughts and feelings dealing with fear.

Good morning! There are a few of you on my timeline God has given a vision for something bigger than where you are! If you're like me, thoughts come at you saying it won't work or you won't be able to do it! Just like they did yesterday for me, as I sat down to continue working on my book. All of a sudden, I heard, "I don't know why you're doing all this work, no one is even going to read it!

Listen, the devil comes to steal every seed of greatness God has ever placed inside of you. Thoughts, voices, and naysayers will come to make you feel defeated, less than, or like you want to quit. But you can't! Not now, not ever. Even if you've taken a temporary pause on your way to your next level of success, pick up where you left off! Your voice, your book, your program, your ideas, your solutions ARE NEEDED, today...not tomorrow! I hope this encourages you as it encouraged me!

The response was overwhelming! People came out of the woodwork thanking me. They all said my post was perfectly timed, and just what they needed to hear! People are waiting on you to accomplish what God called you to do. Find the faith and courage to keep going.

> *God has not given us the spirit of fear, but of power*
> *And love and of a sound mind.*
> • *2 TIMOTHY 1:7 (NKJV)*

Even though I had a glimpse into my future at such a young age, it didn't make the growth process any easier. I had to be prepared for where I am today as well as for what lies ahead. Just as you are in the preparation process for where you will be tomorrow. I still have fears as it relates to success, but they don't hang around for long. For example, I actually had a fear of networking. Most people think that I am an extrovert. *I am not.* It is situational for me. It has taken me a *long* time to get comfortable with and learn the art of networking. I knew that my success would be based on my ability to build strong relationships.

Our vision does not just happen because God has given us a glimpse into our future. We must be matured, groomed, and processed for the full realization of what He has placed in our hearts! When I get frustrated with my own vision because the progress seems to be slow or I appear to be stalling, I am often encouraged by this passage from one of my favorite devotionals.

> *"Sometimes I grant you glimpses of your glorious*
> *future, to encourage you and spur you on. But your*
> *main focus should be staying close to Me. I set the pace*
> *in keeping with your needs and My purposes."*
> - SARAH YOUNG, *JESUS CALLING*

Fear Factor

"When you are in God's ways, you are in His will"
- STEVEN FURTICK

Many people hear God speaking to them, whether it is a whisper or a loud song, but they also fear stepping outside of God's will. Some time ago, I listened to an old message from my pastor, Steven Furtick, called "God's Will is Whatever!" He explained how we ask such big questions like, "God, what if I marry the wrong person? What if I go to the wrong college? What if I move to the wrong city? What if? What if?" While I cannot do justice to the summation of his message, the takeaway was powerful.

Pastor Furtick explained that the only way we can be outside of the will of God is if we are not concerned about His ways. He went on to explain, when we desire what God wants and our heart is pure, He will never let our life get so far off track it would be messed up forever. One decision does not have that much power! Even if it should have been different, it will not ruin your life, especially your destiny forever. He is waiting on you to follow Him knowing that your decision to pursue the vision He gave you is the best decision you could ever make.

COURAGEOUS SPOTLIGHT

ONLY THE STRONG WILL THRIVE

Meet Courageous Joan Randall
Thriving specialist, CEO of Victorious You, Keynote Speaker

M: One Sunday, I was attending my parents' church. Part of the service was the opportunity for Joan to share her story. By the end of her story, I was in tears. I said, "I know I don't know this woman, but I have to go up and meet her and everyone else in the world has to hear her story too." Tell us about what you shared that day.

J: It's hard to speak years of your life into a five-minute testimony. The first thing that came out of my mouth was, "I am a miracle. Standing here before you today is a miracle." When I saw all the things I had gone through and how many times I could have lost my life, I knew that standing in the church that

Sunday, speaking to the congregation was a miracle. I was married to a man who brought me from my home island, Jamaica, to this country. As soon as I got to this country, the physical abuse started. At that time, I had no idea I was experiencing domestic violence. It had gotten to a point where the beatings got so bad that one day he literally kicked me down a flight of stairs in our home and I fell, hit my head, and woke up in the hospital. There was also a time when he was so angry at me for responding to something he said, he turned on the hot water, filled a pan, and poured it on me from my head to my toes.

There were so many instances where I thought he was going to kill me. The most profound moment was when I made up in my mind I was going to take my life. I had it all planned out. When you reach a point in your life that taking your own life, or killing your children is rational, you know you've hit rock bottom. I did not want to live anymore. I could not stand the pain, I cried every night, and I was afraid to share with my family. I was isolated, I couldn't have visitors, and I couldn't have people coming to see me. He disconnected my telephone and there was no home phone. There were times when he would go out of town for a few days and he would turn the gas off so we would have nothing to cook on. I was tired of living that way. I felt guilty that my children were seeing and living this on a daily basis.

I remember the day I was going to take the lives of my children and I. I had a gun and I was sitting on the floor, and my youngest daughter walked in. She walked up to me and said, "Mom, are you sad?" I said, "Yeah, I'm sad." She said, "I can see." Tears were in my eyes. She said, "let me give you strength." I asked her, "What does that mean?" She said, "I can give you strength, I'm going to just hug you and give you strength." She put her arms around me, hugged me, and squeezed me. At that moment, something transferred from my three-and-a-half-year-old daughter into me. I knew, my eyes were opened, as if God was saying, "This is not how I want you to leave this Earth. It's not time." And I knew in that moment I could not take the life of my children nor myself.

I remember having a conversation with my older daughter and saying to her we had to go. She said, "Mom, I've been waiting on this moment for a long time." I said, "What do you mean?" She said, "I've been packing my clothes and my sister's clothes in a bag, and they are in the attic." There in the attic, were six trash bags of clothes for her and her sister for the day when I said to her "Let's go," so she would be ready.

M: I can remember sitting in my seat, listening to you share that story, thinking there is absolutely no way. It reminded me of how God is so amazing, to be able to bring us out of situations and we look nothing like what we've been through. I was looking at a miracle. After you left, you were able to create an amazing career. Tell everyone about that journey.

J: As much as I knew I needed to leave him, I knew in my mind as we put plans in place it was going to be a tough journey. But in my mind at the time, I knew there was a greater power in my life directing my moves with what happened with my daughter. When we finally left, we went to Florida. I had been with my company for about a year or so. I ran away in the middle of the night with my daughters. We stayed in a hotel and called the airlines to purchase three one-way tickets to Florida, where my older sister lived. We went to Florida and stayed for a while. The great thing about my move in all of this was that the company I worked for, understood what I was going through during this period in my life. They got me a transfer from New Jersey to Florida. I felt this sense of relief that in leaving, I would be able to have a job when I got to my destination. In Florida, I was working with the company as a sales associate. Having two daughters and making $7.50 an hour was tough. The good thing was my sister was willing to let us stay with her for a while, until I could get on my feet.

I worked hard, and about six months after I arrived in Florida, I rented a one-bedroom apartment for my two girls and I. I had a part-time job at a grocery store and on the weekends, I took care of sick people on Saturday and Sunday. So here I was juggling three jobs while my seven-year-old was trying to babysit my four-year-old. But it wasn't enough. I still ended up being evicted.

Here I am, nine months later in Florida, homeless with two children. My sister found out and helped me. She reached out to some friends and other people, and got money together for a place to stay. I poured my heart and soul into my work, because that was my release. I started writing in my journals as well. There was nothing else; all I wanted to do was take care of these two little girls. The harder I worked, the more it was recognized. I went into an assistant store management training program, and then became a manager. More promotions started happening. Needless to say, 20 or so years later, I was promoted to a vice-president.

M: So you went from coming from a completely different country, to going through the worst situation imaginable, finding yourself without even a place to stay in Florida, but still maintaining your work ethics. Now, not only do you have the most amazing career, tell us about your love life?

J: God took me from, and this is going to sound really corny, but He took me from the pits to the palace. I never imagined I would ever find someone to truly love me as a queen. But when you give it all to God and let him lead you, that is what happens. For 15 years, I stayed to myself with my two daughters, because I didn't want to have anyone come into their lives and repeat what happened with my first husband. God heard and answered my prayer. I had a very good friend I worked with and that friendship turned into an amazing courtship, that courtship turned into an engagement, that engagement turned into a marriage, and it is absolutely unbelievable!

M: Such a story of redemption. What are you doing now?

J: I'm bursting with excitement to talk about this. The reason why I call myself a thriving specialist is because of Melissa Nixon. I always called myself a survivor, because I survived domestic violence. But when I really think about it, after I met you and we had conversations, where I am today is a result of you. You were the angel God sent into my life to help me walk into my destiny. Our meeting was not by chance, it was divine. I could be in the same place a year ago had I not met you. So what I'm doing now, and the elevation to where I am from where I was a year ago is as a result of Melissa Nixon and God's divine power.

You and I kept in close contact. You said, there's a book inside of you." I said, "Yeah, I have this idea about bags in the attic." And you said to me, "Buy the domain! Buy the domain name today! Don't wait. It doesn't matter when you write the book, buy the domain name now." Every conversation I had with you, you shared something else about courage to me. As a result of you sharing, it might just be one little nugget of information; you have no idea how small that seed was. But every time you and I talked, it was as if God was watering what you were sowing into me. As a result of that, things started to bloom inside. I got pregnant with all of these ideas. I started thinking, you know, "I'm no longer surviving. Surviving is when you come out of some bad situation and you're just living. Now, I've gone past surviving and I'm thriving!

God wants me to walk in my destiny and he has something bigger for me than what I even thought I had inside of me. I bought my domain name, I listened to everything you said to me and more. My life has changed drastically! Today, I've started my own company; I'm founder and CEO of

Victorious You. Our goal is to empower and encourage women who have gone through these types of situations to help and show them they can go from being broken to brave, from being victims to victors. To let them know that, by faith, you can unleash and really birth everything that's within you, everything that God intended you to be. It's amazing what's happening to me.

M: I want people to realize how you got to this point. The most powerful thing you did over and over again, is you said yes. Yes, I'll leave. Yes, I'll start. Yes, I'll restart. Yes, I'll go get the domain name. Yes, I'll start my business. Yes, I'll be courageous enough to tell someone the most intimate things that have ever happened to me. I want people to know your future is contingent upon those three letters.

J: Absolutely. One of the things I always say to myself since I met you was not only "Y-E-S", but just knowing that God wants you to take the first step. All I had to do was take one step. And He has given me 999 steps that has moved me forward from one step to 1000 steps ahead.

M: Living your most courageous life is not about you going and doing the most courageous, radical thing you could ever think of. It is about getting started.

Facing unbelievable life circumstances, Joan literally faced the fear of death, yet found the courage to change her circumstances. Like me, when faced with overwhelming odds, Joan turned to God for direction and strength. He provided everything she needed along the way. The road was tough at first, but in the end she went from victim to victor. Leaping from your career to your calling is a fearful experience on many levels. Yet, being relentless about the pursuit of it will help you to thrive at your newest level.

Fear Facetime

Just know, you will have fear, but it should not be based on the fear of living in regret or never starting. Instead, focus on finally allowing yourself the opportunity to trust God enough to let Him take control of your dreams. Allowing all of your "what ifs" to get in your way should not distract you from allowing your faith questions to pave a way towards your dreams. Here are some examples of common fear-based questions and faith-based answers:

Fear-Based Questions	Faith-Based Answers
What if it doesn't work?	With God all things are possible: **Matthew 19:26**
What if I start and can't go any further?	God's promises are "Yes" and "Amen": **2 Corinthians 1:20**
What if others don't like it?	God can do more than you can ask or think: **Ephesians 3:20**
What if I don't have enough money?	
What if I don't have enough people?	Whatever you ask in prayer, if you believe it will come to pass: **Mark 11:24**
What if consumers don't respond?	You will be blessed if you do not walk in the counsel of the ungodly: **Psalm 1:1**
What if they say "no"?	
What if God doesn't answer my prayers?	God's strength is all you need: **Philippians 4:13 & Isaiah 41:10**
What if I can't take care of my family?	God's word is truth and life: **John 14:6 & John 8:32**

Once you address your fear-based questions with God's faith-based answers, the space between fear and faith will get smaller. You are operating on the spectrum between contentment and extraordinary vision, between little faith and radical faith.

A Willingness to Do What it Takes

Many people will only see the outcome of all your hard work. Rarely will anyone see the long days, long nights, numerous emails sent, phone calls made, or the hundreds of "no's" you received. Nor will they see your list of weekly mundane tasks that sometimes seem to have no purpose, but must be finished, anyway. However, I soon realized that before I hit any major stage, landed any major corporate contracts, or acquired coaching clients, **all of the above** was part of the job description.

STOMPING OUT STEP #11

Note to Fear: You're Fired!

There is no place for paralyzing fear in your courageous leap. God's word has an answer for any challenge or insecurity you come up against. Fear is natural, but it is up to you to tear it down daily with prayer and steadfast belief.

COURAGEOUS STEP #12

LEAP!

If there is one thing I know for sure, it's that there is nothing like a man or a woman with a made up mind! It unleashes a yearning so deep that it makes you feel like you are ready to take on the world. It is scary, exciting, exhilarating, and filled with all kinds of emotions that make you want to accomplish your wildest dreams and thoughts right NOW!

There are so many people like you with a desire in their heart to take a big leap from what they are doing now. Whether your leap is to move up in your career or move out of it, start a business, or take your existing business to the next level, the good news is that you have finally made the decision to say "Yes."

Since God gave you the vision, He expects you to carry it out. God's ways and thoughts are beyond our comprehension, so He knows you better than you know yourself. Nearly all of the examples of chosen vessels in His word were ordinary people with struggles and imperfections like all of us. Therefore, your vision can only be carried out by you, and God will hold you accountable to it.

It's time to move forward with consistency, determination, and faith that the plan is in His hands and you are the chosen vehicle He is using to carry it out. Quitting is not an option, because at some point you realize that it is no longer about you, but about the responsibility God has given you. Believe in the vision you have been given, not the present circumstances that make you comfortable!

Trusting God's plan can be a peaceful and joyous place when we finally stop fighting against both Him and ourselves. It opens up a space inside where you begin to realize that your ideas are not crazy, but are actually graciously given to you by the Creator Himself. You start boldly walking in faith knowing that anything that is God-ordained *will work*!

It is a place where you begin to *believe in* the God you say you serve, instead of just serving Him in name only. The moment you begin to leap from your career to your calling is the precise time that you are willing to wrestle and fight for your faith. If He did it for countless others, there is no doubt He will do it for you.

As you take this leap, just remember that dreams are born one day at time, one dollar at a time, and one step at a time. Time is going to pass whether you start today or tomorrow. Live your life so that you don't wake up and wish you started the thing God placed on your heart the day He gave it to you. Don't live with regrets. Instead, look forward to spending your latter years telling your children, grandchildren, and others the great things that you did do, rather than sharing teachable moments of the things you wish you had done. You've already taken one courageous step. Now stand tall, take a deep breath, and leap into your destiny!

Afterword

"Oh my gosh, you're doing so great Melissa!" is often what I heard in the beginning stages of my entrepreneurial journey. From the snapshot of one picture on social media, things appear that way. However, if a picture is worth one thousand words, then my social media posts only make up five of those words. What they did not see is that rest of the 995 words were the prayers, tears, hard work, and encouragement, all working together to capture that one moment in time. As I continue to impact more and more lives around the world, I now understand that the *Courageous Life* is real. It requires so much of me, yet it is totally worth every ounce of my blood, sweat and tears.

Almost two years into my journey, I met with a former co-worker. She, like many, have watched and cheered from afar, sending virtual support along the way. Our conversation was amazing and I gave her the most transparent answers about my journey to date – hard work, sacrifice, long days and sleepless nights. But there was one question she asked, where I cut her off before getting the complete word out. "Melissa, do you regr.. ?" I mean it, before she could finish sounding out the word "regret," my answer was a resounding "no!"

Taking a career leap fine tunes everything about who you are and how you operate. It is a mindset and personality shift. Turning back is no longer an option, it's non-negotiable. It's no longer a dream, it's your life. Doubts of "will this work?" are replaced with empowering thoughts like "when this works…" It's no longer my ability to only have faith and trust in God when things are comfortable, but having faith and trusting in God, when things are totally uncomfortable. Somewhere along the walk, you honestly believe that moving from your career to your calling is no longer a pipe dream, but the very reason you were created in the first place!

"For the vision is yet for an appointed time; But at the end it will speak, and it will not lie. Though it tarries, wait for it; because it will surely come, It will not tarry."
- HABAKKUK 2:3

Acknowledgments

To my mom, the one person I was nervous to share my courageous leap with years ago, thank you for unwavering love, support, and prayers.

To Jedidah and Jeff, my biggest cheerleaders, thank you for not only continuously cheering me on, but for always reminding me what it means to walk by faith.

To Lana and Marc, you guys are an answer to prayer. Not only do you keep me organized, you are a Godsend that has changed my life.

To Mia, this book is one of the many things due to the result of many weekly prayers over the past few years. Thank you for being my friend and prayer partner.

To Jenni, Misty, Jade, Elizabeth, Jennifer, Jedidah, and Joan thank you for sharing your courageous stories to inspire others to create their own.

To all of my friends that have prayed for and encouraged me...THANK YOU!

To my book coach and editor, Kary Oberbrunner and Kim Rouse, thank you for such an amazing covenant connection during this process. So much more to come.

About the Author

Melissa J. Nixon took the leap from her to career to her calling - to ignite courage in others. Through her writing, speaking, and coaching, she helps individuals and organizations identify and make their next courageous move. Creating a plan to eliminate courage blockers in the process.

As Melissa climbed her corporate career she found herself struggling to own her voice, own her seat at the table, and most importantly own her dream. It wasn't until she realized she was missing two core elements, belief and courage, did things change. Now as a keynote speaker, trainer, executive leadership coach, and Courageous Life Strategist, she spends her time traveling and speaking to help others live courageously as well. She is the Founder of the Courageous Life Academy, a coaching and consulting firm, where she specializes in helping her clients in three core areas 1) excelling in their current career 2) transitioning from their career to their calling and 3) growing their existing business.

Melissa is also a contributing author to the Huffington Post, Addicted 2 Success, and the Network for Executive Women. She holds a MBA in Organization Development and resides in Charlotte, NC. She can often be found exploring her next courageous adventure with her friends and family. If you're ready to start living and leading courageously, visit courageouslifeacademy.com

Her motto is: "I'm not afraid of failure, but I am afraid of regret!"

Stay Connected

Whether you are ready to take the leap or have already taken the leap, I want to know how you're doing! Let's take this journey together. Here's how:

Email us your praise party wins at **hello@courageouslifeacademy.com**

Connect and share your feedback and comments with us online on. Be sure to tag us in pics and posts of you in action living your most courageous life!
    Facebook – Courageous Living with Melissa J. Nixon
    Twitter/Instagram @melissajnixon
    LinkedIn - linkedin.com/in/melissajnixon

Visit us online to inquire about our coaching programs, register for an online course or live event at courageouslifeacademy.com

Celebrate Others - Know someone, living their most courageous life? We would love to feature them as a Courageous Spotlight. Send us a brief email with their background and how they are living their most courageous life to hello@courageouslifeacademy.com

Resources

A great way to make your leap is to reach out to local and national organizations designed to help business owners with every step of the entrepreneurial process. Check out the list below and do your research:

1) **SCORE** - score.org
   Mission: Foster vibrant small business communities through mentoring and education.

2) **Minority Women Business Enterprise** mwbe.com
   Mission: Provide nationwide services to minority and women businesses to educate, mentor, and help leverage their capabilities to maximize opportunities and promote sustainability.

3) **Small Business Administration** sba.gov
   Mission: To deliver millions of loans, loan guarantees, contracts, counseling sessions, and other forms of assistance to small business.

4) **Minority Business Development Agency** mbda.gov
   Mission: Promotes growth and competitiveness of U.S. minority-owned business

5) **Minority Supplier Development Council** nmsdc.org
   Mission: The National Minority Supplier Development Council advances business opportunities for certified minority business enterprises and connects them to corporate members.

6) **Women's Business Enterprise National Council** wbenc.org
   Mission: To fuel economic growth globally through access to opportunities, by identifying, certifying and facilitating development of
   women-owned businesses.

Bring Melissa Into Your Business or Organization

Keynote Speaker. Trainer. Author
Courageous Life Strategist

As a keynote speaker and trainer, Melissa knows what it's like to sit through long presentations and less than impactful trainings. A person's expertise does not always translate into energy and transformation, and Melissa brings both. Her engaging and inspiring style charges each audience to take action and get results. Whether she is speaking about leadership, business, or life management, each person leaves ready to take their next courageous step. Melissa regularly speaks at corporations, colleges, major conferences, and events within the U.S. and abroad.

Connect with Melissa today at
courageouslifeacademy.com

Made in the USA
Charleston, SC
16 August 2016